Navigating the Harris Family Story

Tracing the Ancestry of George and Elizabeth Harris of Battle Creek, Michigan

David J. Harris

John Chapter 1

1 In the beginning was the Word, and the Word was with God,
and the Word was God.
3 Through Him all things were made. Without Him nothing was made that has been made.
14 The Word became flesh and dwelt among us...
He was full of grace and truth.

Table of Contents

Introduction. 5
Chapter 1 George Clark Harris (Father) 7
Chatper 2 Ida Elizabeth Swainston (Harris) (Mother) 11
Chapter 3 Bessie's Letter from 1955 19
Chapter 4 Memories From Our Life on the Farm (1947-1967) 21
Chapter 5 Laura Anne Bell (Grandmother) 27
Chapter 6 John Simpson Swainston (Grandfather) 31
Chapter 7 Laura Anne Swainston (Mother's sister) 33
Chapter 8 Donald John Swainston (Mother's brother) 36
Chapter 9 Robert Holbrook Harris (Father's Brother) (Uncle Bob) 38
Chapter 10 Joseph Harris (Grandfather) (Grandpa Joe) 46
Chapter 11 Joseph Harris & Lenah Williams (GGF) 53
Chapter 12 Isaac & Ann Harris (GGGF) plus descendants. 57
Chapter 13 Ada Hazel Clark (Grandmother) 60
Chapter 14 Cornelia Johnson Snyder (GGM) 63
Chapter 15 William D. Snyder (GGGF) 68
Chapter 16 Eliza (Elizabeth) Jane Brown (GGGM) 75
Chapter 17 Children of William D. Snyder and Eliza Brown 81
Chapter 18 The Threads of Baseball and Enterprise: Our Link to Peck & Snyder 86
Chapter 19 Kirk Reunion 88
Chapter 20 Nehemiah Brown Jr. (GGGGF) 92
Chapter 21 Sarah Purdy – First Wife of Nehemiah Brown Jr. 94
Chapter 22 Betsy (Elizabeth) Second Wife of Nehemiah Brown Jr. (GGGGM) 95
Chapter 23 Descendants of Nehemiah Brown Jr. (GGGGM) 97
Chapter 24 Brown Homestead 1906 106
Chapter 25 James M. Clark (GGF) 111
Chapter 26 Chauncy Clark & Mary Corwin (GGGF) 113
Chapter 27 Hulet H. Clark (GGGGF) 117
Chapter 28 Mary Hallock Clark (GGGGM) - A Life Remembered 120
Chapter 29 Origins of Clarks in America 123
Chapter 30 Clark Genealogy 126
Chapter 31 Southold Exodus (Escaping the British) 133
Chapter 32 Southold Long Island Families 138
Chapter 33 When They Came to America 145
Chapter 34 Cemeteries & Headstones – a Testimony 148
About the Author 149

Introduction

There will be errors in this book as it is still a work in progress. It is also not complete as there are family lines that end up as dead ends, where I can find no further information. Those pieces of this puzzle are missing and waiting to be found.

All the biographies in this book are my direct ancestors. At this moment, I have two great-grandchildren - Cody and Molly Gray. As I write this, I think of you and all those others who carry our family legacy. All of the biographies in this book are your ancestors as well. In them you will find an ancestor born in a debtor's prison, an ancestor who lost five siblings and a mother all within two weeks, ancestors who were in the Revolutionary War, ancestors who were the first settlers of Southold, Long Island, Bedford, NY, Stanford, CT, and Middletown, NY. You will also find an ancestor who was a premier Bass fisherman who invented fishing tackle and fished all over Illinois, Wisconsin, Michigan, Missouri, and Colorado. The work of a genealogist is to gather up all the threads of successive generations of a family and weave them into a harmonious web whose pattern shows not only the characteristics of each family but their progress in the age in which they lived.

To gather these threads is no small task. When gathered, the reward of having rescued them from oblivion is extremely satisfying. Every generation has its challenges in finding these threads. Records before censuses, written histories, directories, birth and death records, newspapers and even headstones, vary by generation and location. When a window opens it becomes an opportunity for continued perseverance.

This history of our family covers a period of almost four hundred years and covers the entirety of the history of our country. Each generation played a part in the development of our nation.

My journey into the discovery of family genealogy began shortly after the death of my grandfather, Joseph Harris, in 1966, over 50 years ago. It started with an old (1854) Welch family Bible, an autograph book once in the possession of my grandmother, Ada, and a McGuffey 5th grade reader with several addresses in it. These, along with incomplete stories from my father, George Harris, Uncle Robert Harris, and their cousin Lucille (Mitchell) Mudgett, became the foundation for this long journey that has not ended. This was a time before computers and the internet, so progress was very slow as most of the work was completed through the mail or traveling to a specific location.

This is not my biography, but the biographies of George and Elizabeth (Swainston) Harris and their ancestors. My goal was to trace every family line back to the time of their arrival in America. This also covers all male and female ancestry lines, not just Harris or Swainston.

On the Swainston side you will read about John Simpson Swainston and Laura Anne Bell. These are short ancestry charts as John and Laura were both born in England. On the Harris side is Joseph Harris and Ada Clark. Joseph's tree is slightly larger as Joseph came from Wales in the 1850s. Many siblings came over as well as his parents. Ada's tree is so big that I divided it between her parents James M. Clark and Cornelia J. Snyder. The Snyder tree is large, but the James Clark tree is extremely large going back to before 1640 in America.

My prayer is that Cody, Molly, and all of my descendants who find and read this work, now having learned about your family history, will each endeavor to make your own mark on this world – to follow the steps of Grandma Swainston and make your faith in Jesus a central point of your life, to follow in the steps of Grandpa John and sail into the unknown, and to follow in the steps of Chauncy Clark and persevere in the face of overwhelming personal losses. To you descendants, I dedicate this work.

David J. Harris

Chapter 1

George Clark Harris

George Clark Harris, the eldest son of Joseph and Ada (Clark) Harris, was born Feb 17, 1910 in Chicago, Illinois. George's brother Robert joined the family in 1912. When George was four years old, the family moved to Battle Creek, Michigan.

The Harris family rented a 2.5 story home on Main Street conveniently located so Joseph could take a leisurely half-mile walk to his work at Grand Trunk. Thankfully, the house was fairly large because living with the Harris four were George's grandmother Cornelia Clark, (Ada's mother), and Cornelia's two spinster sisters, Florence and Wilhelmina. George and Robert shared a bedroom on the top floor, or more precisely, the attic. Both boys loved camping and were active in the Boy Scouts.

George dropped out of high school, before graduating, to begin working. He often remarked he wished he had gone to college and had become an engineer. When George was twenty years old, he met Elizabeth Swainston at a dance. She was fifteen, which was not nearly as creepy then as it is now. Coincidentally, Elizabeth's younger sister, Laura Swainston, was dating George's younger brother Bob (Robert) at the time. Elizabeth's mother, Laura, did not approve of George. Consequently, George and Elizabeth waited until Elizabeth was 21 before getting married on Valentine's Day, February 14, 1937, in Lansing, Michigan - officiated by their former pastor. They attended the First Methodist Church in Battle Creek and were involved in the YMCA.

Ten months after the wedding, George Jr. arrived. James Donald came along two years later. John Raymond was born five years after James with David Joseph arriving two years after John. All the boys were born in Oaklawn Hospital in Marshall. George and Elizabeth moved several times in their first ten years of marriage. They lived with Elizabeth's parents for a couple years at 88 Calhoun Street. They lived at 17 Euclid and 13 Fairview Avenue before moving to 46 Charlotte Street in Battle Creek.

George worked at several different places. Jobs were hard to find during the depression and war era with George being the victim of several plant layoffs and closings. He worked at the Grand Trunk Roundhouse, Nichols and Shepard, United Steel & Wire, Olivers, Eaton (Marshall), Ronan & Kunzel (Marshall), Post Cereal, and other places. He had second jobs including, at one time, refinishing wood floors. George retired as a machine repairman at Eaton Corporation in Battle Creek. George never served in the military because he had dependent children and worked for a company with a military contract. George had a temper and often used foul language. Most days you could hear him swearing, usually at some piece of misbehaving equipment. Those who worked with George would describe him as a short man dressed in green work clothes who smoked a pipe and could swear up a storm.

When he was 36 years old, George and Elizabeth purchased a hundred-acre farm, halfway between Battle Creek and Marshall. Farming became his second job. His ability to repair machinery came in handy on the farm. The farm equipment was all purchased secondhand. George loved to go to auctions and would usually take one of the boys. After six years on the farm an unexpected surprise arrived for the aging couple, another baby boy, their fifth. Even so, William Kenneth was warmly welcomed into the family. Elizabeth, who had been working at Kellogg company, decided to stay at home with her new arrival.

The eldest son, George Jr., gave up farming one year after graduating from high school. The family farm waned a bit as they stopped collecting milk and raising pigs. They still raised calves to show at the fair, beef cattle, chickens, and crops. By posting a sign by the road, the family sold baled hay, straw, butter, and sweet corn for a whopping 25¢/dozen! With the milk cows gone, more time was spent crop farming and working neighboring farmland. This also meant George had more opportunity to use his colorful vocabulary as more equipment would be breaking down. At least seven different neighbors benefitted by George helping plant or harvest hay, straw, wheat, or oats.

The Harris family loved to entertain friends and family by inviting them to the farm. The family would have picnics with grandparents, aunts, uncles, second cousins, and friends. Once during a picnic at a local county park, George scaled the beams of the one lane bridge and balance walked, Wallenda style, over the river. George usually did the grilling which was the only cooking he did. As he grilled, he would sing a song with the unfamiliar lyrics, "They're all red ready, and they're all red hot, with an onion in the middle and a pickle on top!" At the picnics, the kids were often kept busy by cranking the ice cream churn. Homemade ice cream was a favorite and was also affordable as milk, cream and eggs were plentiful on the farm.

One of George's favorite foods was oyster stew. He could consume a can of sardines with soda crackers by himself. He ate leftover cold fish, whether bluegills or smelt, right out of the refrigerator. He would occasionally drink a beer but didn't keep any in the house. He did like Mogen David wine. He loved to smoke his pipe as well, he used the "Velvet" brand of tobacco. George owned the farm for exactly twenty-one years, from 1947 to 1968. In 1968, they moved into a new ranch style house built in the small woods on the southeast corner of the farm. The remainder of the farm was sold in parcels.

In the spring of 1963, George purchased a two-bedroom cottage on Nottawa Lake, south of Marshall. The rustic cottage had no electricity. The family used an outside toilet and a hand pump for water. There were ten cottages on the east side of the lake. For three summers, Harris weekends were spent fishing, swimming, and skiing. George built a pontoon boat for fishing and swimming. On one eventful voyage, there were about twenty people on that homemade pontoon, all headed to a sandbar on the east shore. Suddenly, the overweight load started shifting. A few wise people jumped off to avoid flipping the imperiled craft. The cottage was sold after the summer of 1966 because the cottage was on leased land and the newly constructed interstate, I-69, cut off access to the cottage. Later in the early 1970s, George and his son Jim built a two-bedroom cottage on Podunk Lake, north of Hastings.

For years George drove a blue Chevrolet El Camino with a three-speed column shift. He didn't need all three speeds as he never used first gear. He drove his car like he drove his tractor.

George and Elizabeth were active in the local Farm Bureau. Once a month the group would get together for a card party, most often at the Harris residence. They always played Pedro. Elizabeth usually served her shrimp salad.

George did not attend church except on the major religious holidays of Easter or Christmas or when there was a potluck. He never talked about what he believed spiritually. In his later years, it was not uncommon to see him with tears in his eyes as he watched Billy Graham on TV. At least once he secretly paid for a load of coal to be delivered to a household who was having difficulty. Once, Elizabeth had a discussion with her son David about the importance of tithing. She decided to try it. But, how would she approach George in this step of faith? George, somewhat surprisingly, never said a word against it.

George retired when he was 65. He started sharpening mower blades, saw blades, and chainsaws. He also started playing golf. George was born right-handed but injured his arm playing ball as a youth, so he converted to a southpaw. While he did everything left-handed, when it came to golf, he played right-handed but took the unusual tack of using a cross handed grip. That is most likely the reason George had a "hard time" keeping score.

When he was 75, George became sick at home and went to his doctor. Foolishly, the doctor would not admit him to the hospital. Finally, a few days later, the doctor admitted him for dehydration. Within 36 hours, on October 28, 1985, George died from an electrolyte imbalance. He is buried with his wife, parents, and extended family at Memorial Park Cemetery in Battle Creek, Michigan.

Figure 1. Elizabeth and George Harris

Chapter 2

Ida Elizabeth Swainston (Harris)

It was a rainy day in New York City, February 6, 1915, when John Swainston looked into the face of his firstborn, a daughter, and said, "We'll name her Ida, after my only sister." John's wife Laura agreed but only, "As long as we can give her the middle name of Elizabeth, after my sister." With such attention to her name, it's interesting that Ida Elizabeth Swainston would be called Bessie by her family. Once married, the more mature Bessie decided that Elizabeth was a more appropriate moniker.

John and Laura, immigrants from South Shields, England, gave birth to Laura, Bessie's little sister, when Bessie was two. With a growing family, John and Laura decided it would be nice to live closer to relatives, so they decided to move closer to John's aunt Mary (Allen), Uncle Thomas Swainston, and cousins who were living in Battle Creek, Michigan. So, when Bessie was three, the family headed west to Battle Creek. Once settled, Bessie's only brother Donald was born in 1919.

Like many immigrants at that time, the Swainstons worked hard but did not have much. Struggling financially, they often moved from one rental house to another. They were poor, but they were proud. Laura instilled in her children the charge, "We might be poor, but we don't have to dress like we are poor." Bessie, Laura, and Donald were well known as sharp, snappy dressers. Donald even wore a suit to school most days.

The Swainston family were church goers. As teens, the church youth group hosted a Halloween party. John and Laura were happy to send their daughters, Bessie, 15, and Laura, 13, to this fun, safe social event. That night at the party, the Swainston girls met the Harris boys, George and Robert. The Swainston girls needed a ride home after the party that night. George had a car. At 20 years old, he was naturally old enough to drive. His brother Robert, then 18, tagged along. Despite their age difference, Robert wasted no time and started dating Laura. A short time later, George and Bessie were dating.

Bessie was a wonderful student. She excelled in the classroom, graduating from high school in 1933 as a member of the National Honor Society. After

graduation she found employment at the Cook Coffee Company doing accounting. A couple of years later, she was promoted and moved to Grand Rapids. At this time, she had made plans to marry George Harris who was still living and working in Battle Creek. They would correspond by letters and, when possible, she would return to Battle Creek on the weekends. When she was nearly 22, Bessie, now going by Elizabeth, quit her job and married George. They were married in Lansing because their Methodist pastor had moved there.

Elizabeth and George had five boys. George Clark Jr. was born in 1937, named, of course, after his dad. James Donald was born in 1939 and named after his great grandfather James and uncle Don. John Raymond was born in 1944 and named after his grandfather John and Marion Jones' brother Ray. David Joseph was born in 1946 and named after King David and his grandfather Joseph. William Kenneth was born in 1953 and named after William(?) and Ken Jones. Although they lived in Battle Creek, all the boys were born in Marshall as Elizabeth's best friend was Marion Jones, wife of Dr. Tyre Kenneth Jones.

Most of Elizabeth's life was spent raising her five boys. When the oldest, George, was 9, they moved to a 100-acre farm between Battle Creek and Marshall. She worked for a few years at Kellogg's cereal company, dropping rewards into the cereal boxes. She never worked after her last son was born. Her husband George worked at companies like Eaton, Post, and Oliver as a machine repairman and for himself on the farm. Farming in the 1950s was a little different than it is today. They had cows and sold milk to the Pet Milk Company. The family also raised beef cattle, pigs, and chickens. They also did some crop farming. Neither Elizabeth nor George were previously farming people so the decision to buy a farm had more to do with raising their boys than wanting to become farmers. George's dad Joseph (Joe) lived with the family and actually helped purchase the farm and raise the boys. The farm did help produce an income as they sold sweet corn for 25 cents a dozen, fresh eggs, hay, straw and homemade butter, which Elizabeth made.

Elizabeth was a seamstress and sewed for other people. It seems like she was always sewing for her friend Marion, who did pay her. Every Thursday, she and Marion would go shopping together. Elizabeth sewed all the shirts the boys wore and baked many cookies for them. Growing up, the Harris boys were envious of their school friends who owned store-bought shirts and ate store-bought cookies. As grown men, those same boys now know they would rather have their mom's homemade molasses cookies, which are much better than any cookie found in the aisles of a grocery store.

Elizabeth made sure to teach each of her boys how to cook and sew. In the summer, she would can tomatoes, peaches, etc. There were grapes on the farm.

She would make jelly by the pint - always with a paraffin seal and enough to last the entire year. The boys always looked forward to this special jelly-making day as they would fill their bellies slathering jelly on two loaves of toasted bread. Another treat was to put jelly on leftover pie crust which was made with the farm's own lard. Compared to jelly day, cleaning chickens' day was a much less fun family farming activity.

Elizabeth and George did not travel much while raising their five boys but did have a lot of picnics. The Harris family made County Park, which is two miles south of Michigan Avenue on Wattles Road, a popular picnic spot during the 1950s. When not at the park, the side yard of the farm made for a great picnic location. Picnics always included family like Grandma and Grandpa Swainston, Grandpa Joe, Robert Harris and his daughter Becky, as well as family friends like the Dr. and Marion Jones family, the Mudgett family of Lucille, Al, and Ralph, Ray Machee, and Earl and Reva Squires. George and Elizabeth could never afford the luxury of a camera, but many friends including Dr. Jones and Uncle Bob made 8 mm videos. Every year, Dr. Jones would take the family photo which was then used for their Christmas cards.

In the early 60s, pizza became popular. Sunday nights on the farm were spent making pizza and popcorn. The pizza was always made on a 9x13 cookie sheet and topped with polish sausage and canned mushrooms.

Elizabeth, a godly woman, had a deep faith in Jesus Christ and was a great example to others. She was always active in her church and Women Society group. She was awarded a Life Membership for her service. She had the routine of getting up before anyone else, going to the basement to stoke up the coal furnace, then reading her Bible and doing devotions before anyone else got up. While they lived on the farm, she attended Convis Union Methodist Church. Every Sunday she expected Grandpa Joe and the boys to go to Sunday School and church services with her. Four of the five boys found wives at that little church. Elizabeth's husband George only attended church occasionally, but he did approve of her church activities.

Figure 2. Elizabeth with some of her grandchildren (abt. 1998)
(Mark, Jimmy, Mary Carol, Amy, Joe, Roger)

Descendants of George Clark Harris & Elizabeth Swainston

Generation 1

1.   **GEORGE CLARK[1]HARRIS** was born on 17 Feb 1910 in Chicago, IL. He died on 28 Oct 1985 in Battle Creek, MI (certificate). He married Ida Elizabeth Swainston, daughter of John Simpson Swainston and Laura Anne Bell on 14 Feb 1937 in Lansing, MI. She was born on 06 Apr 1915 in New York, NY. She died on 06 Dec 2007 in Battle Creek, MI.

George Clark Harris and Ida Elizabeth Swainston had the following children:

2.   i.   GEORGE CLARK HARRIS JR. was born on 18 Dec 1937 in Marshall, MI.
3.   ii.   JAMES DONALD HARRIS (Jim) was born on 23 Oct 1939 in Marshall, MI.
4.   iii. JOHN RAYMOND HARRIS was born on 12 Aug 1944 in Marshall, MI.
5.   iv.   DAVID JOSEPH HARRIS was born on 20 July 1946 in Marshall, MI.
        v.   WILLIAM KENNETH HARRIS (Bill)was born on 08 Sep 1953 in Marshall, MI.

Generation 2 (George & Elizabeth's children)

2.   **GEORGE CLARK[2] HARRIS JR.** was born on 18 Dec 1937 in Marshall, MI. He died on 15 Apr 1999 in Vermontville, MI. He married (1) **LINDA ROSANNE STAGE** on 28 June 1959 in Battle Creek, MI. She was born on 24 Jun 1939 in Marshall, MI. He married (2) **JUDY HIGGENBOTHAM** on 22 Sep 1984 in Harrisburg, Illinois. She was born on 16 Feb 1947.

George Clark Harris Jr. and Linda Rosanne Stage had the following children:

6.   i.   ROGER CLARK[3] HARRIS was born on 10 Apr 1960 in Battle Creek, MI.
7.   ii.   MARY CAROL HARRIS was born on 12 Sep 1961 in Battle Creek, MI.

3.   **JAMES DONALD[2] HARRIS (Jim)** was born on 23 Oct 1939 in Marshall, MI. He married
(1) **SUSAN PARROTT** about 1963 in Battle Creek, MI. He married (2) **ANNA MARIE ZERGEOTIS** on 07 Oct 1967 in Battle Creek, MI. She was born on 11 Jan 1939 in Battle Creek.

James Donald Harris and Anna Marie Zergeotis had the following children:
8.   i.   JAMES DONALD[3] HARRIS was born on 08 Feb 1969 in Battle Creek, MI.
9.   ii.   JULIE ANN HARRIS was born on 21 Feb 1972 in Battle Creek, MI.

4.   **JOHN RAYMOND[2] HARRIS** was born on 12 Aug 1944 in Battle Creek, MI. He married (1) **BARBARA JEAN HUYCK** in May 1965 in Battle Creek, MI. She was born on 06 Dec 1946 in Marshall, MI. He married (2) **BARBARA ANN GUSTAFSON** on 04 Sep 1970 in Marshall, MI. She was born on 03 Dec 1946 in Chicago, IL.

John Raymond Harris and Barbara Jean Huyck had the following children:

10.   i.   JACK MICHAEL[3] GREEN was born on 05 Jan 1968. He married THERESA J. O'SULLIVAN.

11.   ii.   JILL SHANNON GREEN was born on 15 May 1970. She married JAMES FLEMING.

John Raymond Harris and Barbara Ann Gustafson had the following children:

12.   iii.   JOSEPH JOHN HARRIS was born on 22 Jul 1973 in Marshall, MI.

13.   iv.   DAWN MARIE HARRIS was born on 23 Apr 1974 in Marshall, MI.

5.   **DAVID JOSEPH**[2] **HARRIS** was born on 20 July 1946 in Marshall, MI. He married Mary Ann Keathley on 23 Sep 1967 in Battle Creek, MI. She was born on 01 Aug 1946 in Battle Creek, MI.   David Joseph Harris and Mary Ann Keathley had the following children:

14.   i.   MARK DAVID[3] HARRIS was born on 03 Aug 1969 in Battle Creek, MI.

15.   ii.   AMY MARIE HARRIS was born on 24 July 1972 in Battle Creek, MI.

Generation 3 (grandchildren, and great grandchildren)

6.   **ROGER CLARK**[3] **HARRIS** (George Clark[2] Jr) was born on 10 Apr 1960 in Battle Creek, MI. He married Cynthia Ann Locke, daughter of John Edward Locke and Judeth Ann Ludwig on 16 May 1985 in Charlotte, Michigan. She was born on 19 Jan 1962 in Charlotte, Michigan. She died on 24 Dec 2015 in Charlotte, Michigan.   Roger Clark Harris and Cynthia Ann Locke had the following children:

16.   i.   JESSE CLARK[4] HARRIS was born on 15 Apr 1986 in Lansing, MI. He married Natalie Kay Anderson on 30 Aug 2014 in Three Rivers, MI. She was born on 27 July 1989 in Kalamazoo, MI.

     ii.   ELIZABETH ANN HARRIS was born on 03 Oct 1988 in Lansing, Michigan. She married Timothy (TJ) Smith on 19 Oct 2013 in Charlotte, mi. He was born on 10 Dec 1989.

17.   iii.   SARAH CHRISTINE HARRIS was born on 28 May 1991 in Lansing, Michigan. She married Chris Johnston on 16 Apr 2016 in Newton, KS.

7.   **MARY CAROL**[3] **HARRIS** (George Clark[2] Jr.) was born on 12 Sep 1961 in Battle Creek, MI. She married Greg Paul Jude Kueppers, son of Frank Charles Kueppers and Patricia Anne Dorr on 16 June 1984 in Holt, MI. He was born on 30 June 1959 in St. Paul, MN.

Mary Carol Harris and Greg Paul Jude Kueppers had the following children:

18.   i.   MICHEL CLARK KUEPPERS was born on 23 Mar 1988 in Lansing, MI. He married Rochelle Otto on 13 Jun 2015 in Mason, MI. She was born on 19 July 1990.

        ii.   JENNIE ELIZABETH KUEPPERS was born on 23 Feb 1990 in Lansing, MI.

8.   **JAMES DONALD**[3] **HARRIS** (James Donald[2]) was born on 08 Feb 1969 in Battle Creek, MI. He married Jennifer Marie Wright on 10 Jul 1999 in Galesburg, MI. She was born on 02 Jan 1972 in Galesburg, MI.

        James Donald Harris and Jennifer Marie Wright had the following child:

        i.   SAMANTHA IRENE MARIE[4] HARRIS was born on 03 May 2001.
           I. Sydney Harris was born 20 Jan 2014 in Battle creek, MI

9.   **JULIE ANN**[3] **HARRIS** (James Donald[2], George Clark[1]) was born on 21 Feb 1972 in Battle Creek, MI. She married **LEVI GORE**. She married (2) **JOHN EDWIN SUPRENANT** on 03 Sep 1999 in Battle Creek, MI. He was born on 12 Dec 1965 in Hamond, IN.

10.   **JACK MICHAEL**[3] **GREEN** (John Raymond[2]) was born on 05 Jan 1968. He married **THERESA J. O'SULLIVAN**.

        Jack Michael Green and Theresa J. O'Sullivan had the following children:

        i.   OLIVA MARIE O'SULLIVAN[4] GREEN was born on 13 Sep 2004 in Norwich, CT.
        ii.   LILLIAN ROSE O'SULLIVAN GREEN was born on 02 May 2007 in Norwich, CT.

11.   **JILL SHANNON**[3] **GREEN** (John Raymond[2] Harris, George Clark[1] Harris,John Raymond[2], George Clark[1] Harris) was born on 15 May 1970. She married **JAMES FLEMING**.

12.   **JOSEPH JOHN**[3] **HARRIS** (John Raymond[2]) was born on 22 July 1973 in Marshall, MI. He married Karla Kirsten Wostrel on 02 Jun 1996 in Rock Springs Wyoming. She was born on 24 Jan 1976 in Norfolk, Nebraska.

        Joseph John Harris and Karla Kirsten Wostrel had the following children:

        i.   ARIANNA MCKENZIE[4] HARRIS was born on 12 Mar 2000 in Marshall, MI.
        ii.   AMBER MARIAH HARRIS was born on 17 Jun 2002.
        iii. BENJAMIN NATHANIAL HARRIS was born on 09 July 2005 in Battle Creek, MI.

13.   **DAWN MARIE**[3] **HARRIS** (John Raymond[2]) was born on 23 Apr 1974 in Marshall, MI. She married (1) **MICHAEL DAVID STALLARD** on 20 Aug 1994 in Battle Creek, MI. She married (2) **BOB SIBAL** on 13 Oct 2012 in Richland, Michigan.

Dawn Marie Harris and Michael David Stallard had the following children:

i.   JOSHUA MICHAEL STALLARD was born on 01 June 1999 in Columbus, OH.
ii.   DESERAY BARBARA MARIEE STALLARD was born on 17 Aug 2003 in Columbus.

14.   **MARK DAVID**[3] **HARRIS** (David Joseph[2]) was born on 03 Aug 1969 in Battle Creek, Michigan. He married Barbara (Barbi) Ann Hill on 31 Oct 1992 in McPherson, Kansas. She was born on 13 Nov 1970 in McPherson, Kansas.

Mark David Harris and Barbara (Barbi) Ann Hill had the following children:

i.   ALBY ANN[4] HARRIS was born on 03 May 1993 in Salina, KS
ii.   GRANT DAVID HARRIS was born on 17 Dec 1996 in Salina, KS
iii. MARLEY ELIZABETH HARRIS was born on 24 Jan 2006 in Salina, KS

15.   **AMY MARIE**[3] **HARRIS** (David Joseph[2]) was born on 24 Jul 1972 in Battle Creek, MI. She married Chad Everett Wallace on 14 Aug 1993 in Battle Creek, MI. He was born on Aug 22, 1972 in Plymouth, Indiana.

Amy Marie Harris and Chad Everett Wallace had the following children:

i.   ALLY MARIE WALLACE was born on 23 May 1998 in Lexington, KY. She married LUKE STEPHEN GRAY on 28 December 2019 in Anderson, Madison, Indiana.
ii.   CARSON EVERETT WALLACE was born on 11 Sep 2001 in Anderson, Indiana. He married Elizabeth Mae Langdon on 20 May 2023 in Muncie, Delaware, Indiana, USA. She was born on 13 Feb 2002.
iii. MASON DAVID WALLACE was born on 14 Oct 2003 in Anderson, Indiana.

Generation 4 (great-great-grandchildren)

16.   **JESSE CLARK**[4] **HARRIS** (Roger Clark[3], George Clark Jr.) was born on 15 Apr 1986 in Lansing, Michigan. He married Natalie Kay Anderson on 30 Aug 2014 in Three Rivers, MI. She was born on 27 Jul 1989 in Kalamazoo, mi.
        Jesse Clark Harris and Natalie Kay Anderson had the following children:
i.   JESSE CLARK[5] HARRIS was born on 07 July 2016 in Charlotte, MI.
ii.   CONNOR ANDERSON HARRIS was born on 21 June 2020.

17.   **SARAH CHRISTINE[4] HARRIS** (Roger Clark[3], George Clark[2] Jr.) was born on 28 May 1991 in Lansing, MI. She married Chris Johnston on 16 Apr 2016 in Newton, KS.

Sarah Christine Harris and Chris Johnston had the following child:
  i.   PEARL CYNTHIA JOHNSTON was born on 30 Oct 2017.

18.   **MICHEL CLARK KUEPPERS** (Mary Carol[3] Harris, George Clark[2] Harris Jr.) was born on 23 Mar 1988 in Lansing, Michigan. He married Rochelle Otto on 13 Jun 2015 in Mason, MI. She was born on 19 July 1990.

Michel Clark Kueppers and Rochelle Otto had the following children:
  i.   LUCILLE JOE KUEPPERS was born on 18 July 2018.
  ii. JOHN PAUL CLARK KUEPPERS was born on 26 Oct 2019

19.   **ALLY MARIE WALLACE** (Amy Marie[3] Harris, David Joseph Harris) was born on 23 May 1998 in Lexington, KY. She married **LUKE GRAY**.

Ally Marie Wallace and Luke Gray had the following children:
  i.   CODY JOSEPH GRAY was born on 09 Apr 2023 in Indianapolis, IN.
  ii. MOLLY ANN GRAY was born on 24 Feb 2025 in Indianapolis, IN

Chapter 3

Bessie's Letter from 1955

In 1986, the year after my father, George Harris died, my mother, Elizabeth (Swainston) Harris, moved from the house they had lived in for 18 years. That house was built on a wooded corner of their farm, where they raised boys. While helping, mother move, I found an old letter written in December of 1955. The letter was still in the sealed, stamped (3 cent) envelope. Mother had set it aside and forgot to send it. It was addressed to a relative (cousin?) in England. She told me to throw it away as it was 30 years old. I kept the letter. Here is what Mother wrote in her letter.

<u>Christmas 1955</u>

We thought perhaps some of our friends would like a newsy letter about our family.

Kenneth (Kenny) was 2 years old on Sept. 8th. He is learning to talk and doing well. Needless to say he is the pride and joy of all of us and we all enjoy him a great deal.

John was eleven in August. He is in the 5th grade at Wattles School and does quite well. He loves to play ball - - any kind, in fact he cries sometimes because David gets tired of playing with him. He can't wait until he is old enough to play on a team. John and David are always wrestling or taking a pop at each other and they are very evenly matched.

David was nine in July. He and John are almost the same size in fact. They are even mistaken for twins at times. David is in the 4th grade and is very good with numbers. The bus takes them both to and from school from almost in front of the house.

James (Jim), who was 16 in October is a Junior in Marshall High School. He does very well in school and always has, even though he takes all of the hard subjects - Latin, Algebra, Chemistry, etc. Of course he has always planned on going to college however he is not sure yet just what he wants to be. He has already started to save for his education. He works after school in the produce dept. At the A&P store in Marshall and seems to enjoy it. He is secretary and treasurer of the Sunday School at the Methodist Church that we go to about 2 miles from home. Jim is quite a serious fellow- not much monkey business with him. He loves cars and studies all about them just for fun. If anyone wants to know anything about them, he can sure tell you. Jim and George have a 49 Mercury which they share.

George Jr. was 18 this month. He is a senior at Marshall High School. He has always been active in the Marshall chapter of the Future Farmers of America (F.F.A.). This year he is the Vice-President of this organization. He has won several honors in his work with the chapter, including a week trip to Kansas City to the National Convention last year and a trip to Illinois this year. He has been on the radio quite frequently and also T.V. He has always been tops in his class with his farm program in which he is very interested. Last year he earned his letter on the reserve football team. George owns nine head of cattle and 2 pigs. He milks four cows before and after school and sells the milk to the Pet Milk Co. This year he raised and sold 27 pigs. With his own corn picker and combine, he earned extra money this summer, all of which he is putting back into the farm. When he is through school in June, he does not want to go to college but thinks he would like to farm in a big way. George is a very active fellow and seems to get a great deal of pleasure out of life. He doesn't seem to mind hard work of which there sure is plenty on a farm. This year George is president of the M.Y.F. youth group at our church.

We have been on the farm now for, going on 9 years and are quite active in the church and community around us. George holds an office in the township government, and we belong to the Emmett Farm Bureau group. George doesn't get to go much now as he is working the second shift at the Eaton Mfg. Co. as a machine repairman. He seems to like his job and does really well.

Me -- right now I just try to keep house and feed these guys. I have a small office in the Women's Society at Church and one in the P.T.A., but while Kenny is small, I have plenty at home to keep me busy.

Grandpa Joe (George's Dad) still lives with us except about 3 months in the winter which he spends in Florida. He is in fairly good health in spite of his 80 years.

We wish you all a very Merry Christmas and a Happy New Year.

- Bessie

Chapter 4

Memories From Our Life on the Farm 1947-1967

In the heart of Michigan, between the bustling towns of Battle Creek and Marshall, a story of family and legacy unfolded in the summer of 1947. George and Elizabeth Harris, seeking a haven for their growing family, laid claim to a sprawling 100-acre farm. This wasn't merely a purchase of land; it was the planting of roots, the beginning of a chapter in the Harris lineage.

George, a man of skilled hands, balanced the demands of a machine repairman in local manufacturing plants with the meticulous craft of refinishing wood floors. His labor, both industrial and artisanal, provided the foundation upon which their farm life would be built. But the farm was more than just a home; it was a sanctuary for George's father and their four sons, a place where the boys could grow strong amidst the rhythm of rural life.

The farmhouse, a testament to mid-19th-century craftsmanship, stood as a silent witness to generations past. Built in the 1850s, it began as a two-story dwelling with three bedrooms nestled beneath its gabled roof. By the time George and Elizabeth arrived, its layout had evolved, reflecting the changing needs of its inhabitants. It now boasted five bedrooms—three upstairs and two downstairs—a spacious eat-in kitchen, a grand dining room, a welcoming living room, a single modest bathroom, a back utility room, and a separate laundry and workroom. A low-ceiling attic, perched above the kitchen, and a coal-filled basement, where the furnace's fuel was stored, hinted at the home's older, simpler days. The chill of Michigan winters, however, still permeated the upstairs and attic, a reminder of the house's unmodernized corners.

The barn, a monument to agricultural enterprise, stood proudly beside the farmhouse. Its expansive hay lofts, both front and back, promised bountiful harvests. Grain storage rooms and five horse stalls on the main level spoke of a time when horses and grain were the lifeblood of the farm. Below, a milking parlor, capable of accommodating up to fifteen cows, and a solitary cement silo for silage, hinted at the farm's dairy potential. Outbuildings, including a well house, pig pen, chicken house, and a garage with an adjoining corn crib, completed the picture of a self-sufficient homestead.

The land itself, a near-perfect square stretching half a mile between the 11-mile and 11 ½-mile roads, was divided into seven large fields, each a canvas for cultivation. In one corner, a small, unassuming woods, less than an acre in size, provided grazing for the livestock. It's quiet presence, however, concealed a secret:

beneath the shade of the hickory trees lay the remnants of a small cemetery, its inhabitants relocated to the Ceresco cemetery in the late 1800s. This forgotten burial ground, a silent echo of the past, added a layer of history to the Harris family's new beginning.

And so, the Harris farm became more than just a place on a map; it became a living chronicle of generations, a testament to the enduring spirit of family, and a tangible link to the rich tapestry of Michigan's rural heritage.

In that autumn of 1947, as the leaves began to turn and the Michigan air grew crisp, the Harris family settled into their new life on the farm. George, the eldest son, was nine, followed by Jim at seven, John at three, and little David, barely a year old. Six years would pass before the arrival of William, affectionately known as Ken, completing the circle of Harris sons. Overseeing this growing brood was Grandpa Joe, a seasoned 72-year-old, whose wisdom and experience anchored the family.

The farm became their world, a boundless playground and a source of endless adventure. Unlike their city-dwelling counterparts, the Harris boys never yearned for summer vacations. The farm itself was their perpetual holiday, a place where work and play intertwined seamlessly. Holidays were grand affairs, filled with boisterous gatherings and sprawling picnics in the side yard, where friends and relatives mingled amidst laughter and shared meals.

The rhythm of farm life soon dictated their days. The milking of cows, a task largely shouldered by George Jr., became a daily ritual. The milk, graded B, was sold to the Pet Milk Company, while the family enjoyed its rich bounty. A cream separator in the back utility room transformed milk into butter, crafted by Elizabeth's skilled hands and sold to neighbors. Eggs, baled hay, straw, and sweet corn, which sold for a humble 25 cents a dozen or a dollar a bushel, were also offered to the community, each contributing to the farm's livelihood.

Unlike the specialized farms of today, the Harris farm embraced a diverse array of agricultural pursuits. Crops were cultivated, cows were milked, and a menagerie of calves, pigs, and chickens thrived. Hay and grain were sold, the latter taken to the elevator for processing. During the years of milking cows, the farm produced hay, corn silage, and ground feed from their own corn and oats. In the early days, before the advent of hay balers, loose hay was hoisted into the barn's lofts using a system of tracks, pulleys, ropes, and hay hooks.

The farm's workhorses were a 1939 Farmall model M tractor and a John Deere model H, the latter requiring a manual flywheel start. The Farmall, capable of pulling a three-bottom plow, was the primary workhorse. A two-row corn picker, combine, baler, manure spreader, hay rake, hay mower, plows, discs, and drags completed the arsenal of farm implements. As technology advanced, newer equipment replaced the old, though most were used and required frequent repairs.

George, their father, possessed an innate drive to work the land, extending his labor beyond the boundaries of their own farm. He found work for neighbors, baling hay, planting, and combining wheat on smaller plots. Their closest neighbor, Powers, entrusted them with the task of putting up hay on his 20-plus acres. Whether it was for payment or simply to maintain the land, the Harris family cultivated a network of neighborly assistance, working with at least eight different landowners over the years.

The Harris farm, therefore, was not just a place of residence, but a vibrant hub of community and industry. It was a place where the rhythms of nature and the bonds of family intertwined, creating a legacy that would endure through generations.

The Harris farm wasn't just a homestead; it was the vibrant heart of a close-knit community. "Neighbors" weren't confined to those living next door; they encompassed everyone within a mile or two, a sprawling network of shared lives and communal joy. Summer brought the crack of bats and the roar of cheering as the ball diamond, initially nestled west of the yard, expanded to a field east of the old pig pen, now vacant. Winter transformed the barn's upper loft into a basketball haven, drawing in neighbors for spirited games. Two small hills provided sledding thrills, while Robert Logan's "Coke a Cola" sign, accommodating three or four riders, turned a larger hill into a winter carnival. Crowley's pond, half a mile south, became a stage for ice skating and hockey, and their fields hosted spirited football matches.

Memories etched in time painted a vivid picture of life on the farm. Backyard picnics, overflowing with laughter and the aroma of grilling food, were a staple. George, their father, would sing his signature tune, "there all red ready, there all red hot, with an onion in the middle and a pickle on top," as he manned the grill. B-B gun battles in the barn, the sweet taste of fresh grape jelly on toast after a day of canning, and the comforting warmth of heat registers after a frigid night upstairs were woven into the fabric of their childhood.

The attic echoed with the rhythmic clatter of ping pong balls, while the barn resonated with the thud of basketballs. The task of catching and cleaning chickens, though grim, was a shared experience. John's daring leaps from the high tree swing, George's acrobatic attempts to swing across the barn, and the inevitable mishaps that led to Doctor Jones's annual stitching sessions, particularly after encounters with the infamous tree swing, became legendary tales.

Summer picnics were enlivened by Becky's impromptu ride on a Holstein cow. Thanksgiving dinners were a riot of flung dinner rolls and upside-down butter plates. The thrill of chasing rabbits in the hayfields, only to release them, and the curious sight of barn cats swimming across the stock tank, added to the farm's unique charm.

Through it all, the Harris farm stood as a testament to the enduring power of family, community, and the simple joys of rural life. It was a place where hard work and hearty laughter intertwined, creating a legacy that would echo through the generations, a story not just of a farm, but of a life well-lived.

Figure 3. Dec. 1957 - George, Jim, John, David, William

Figure 4. Clockwise from top left - David, Jim, John, Elizabeth, William, George

Figure 5. Clockwise from top left - William, David, George, John, Jim, Elizabeth, George

The following pages shows the ancestors of George & Elizabeth Harris. The chapters in this book are written about our ancestors shown on this chart - where possible.

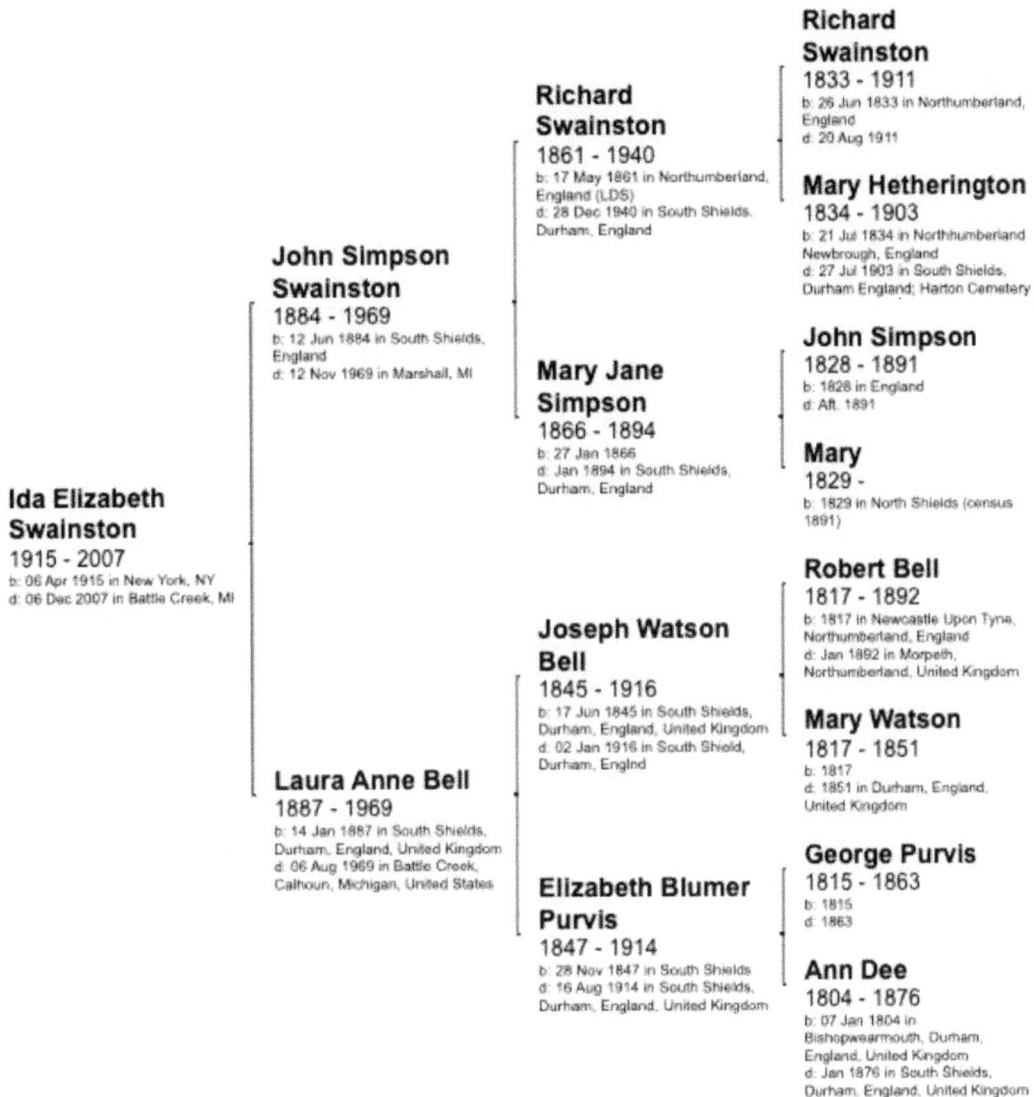

Richard Swainston
1833 - 1911
b: 26 Jun 1833 in Northumberland, England
d: 20 Aug 1911

Richard Swainston
1861 - 1940
b: 17 May 1861 in Northumberland, England (LDS)
d: 28 Dec 1940 in South Shields, Durham, England

Mary Hetherington
1834 - 1903
b: 21 Jul 1834 in Northhumberland Newbrough, England
d: 27 Jul 1903 in South Shields, Durham England; Harton Cemetery

John Simpson Swainston
1884 - 1969
b: 12 Jun 1884 in South Shields, England
d: 12 Nov 1969 in Marshall, MI

John Simpson
1828 - 1891
b: 1828 in England
d: Aft. 1891

Mary Jane Simpson
1866 - 1894
b: 27 Jan 1866
d: Jan 1894 in South Shields, Durham, England

Mary
1829 -
b: 1829 in North Shields (census 1891)

Ida Elizabeth Swainston
1915 - 2007
b: 06 Apr 1915 in New York, NY
d: 06 Dec 2007 in Battle Creek, MI

Robert Bell
1817 - 1892
b: 1817 in Newcastle Upon Tyne, Northumberland, England
d: Jan 1892 in Morpeth, Northumberland, United Kingdom

Joseph Watson Bell
1845 - 1916
b: 17 Jun 1845 in South Shields, Durham, England, United Kingdom
d: 02 Jan 1916 in South Shield, Durham, Englnd

Mary Watson
1817 - 1851
b: 1817
d: 1851 in Durham, England, United Kingdom

Laura Anne Bell
1887 - 1969
b: 14 Jan 1887 in South Shields, Durham, England, United Kingdom
d: 06 Aug 1969 in Battle Creek, Calhoun, Michigan, United States

George Purvis
1815 - 1863
b: 1815
d: 1863

Elizabeth Blumer Purvis
1847 - 1914
b: 28 Nov 1847 in South Shields
d: 16 Aug 1914 in South Shields, Durham, England, United Kingdom

Ann Dee
1804 - 1876
b: 07 Jan 1804 in Bishopwearmouth, Durham, England, United Kingdom
d: Jan 1876 in South Shields, Durham, England, United Kingdom

George Clark Harris
1910 - 1985
b: 17 Feb 1910 in Chicago, IL
d: 28 Oct 1985 in Battle Creek, MI
(certificate)

Joseph Harris
1875 - 1966
b: 05 Mar 1875 in Wiconisco,
Dauphin Co., PA
d: 25 Jun 1966 in Battle Creek, MI
(certificate)

Joseph Harris
1826 - 1886
b: 04 Nov 1826 in Tredegar,
Bedwellty, Monmouthshire, Wales
d: Nov 1886 in Illinois?

Issac Harris
1793 - 1876
b: 1793 in Bedwellty Parish,
Monmouthshire, Wales
d: 1876 in Braceville, Grundy Co.,
IL.

Ann Harris
1804 - 1882
b: Abt. 1804 in Bedwellty Parish,
Monmouthshire, Wales
d: Bef. 1882 in Illinois?

Lenah Williams
1833 - 1885
b: 17 May 1833 in Llanhilleth,
Bedwellty, Monmouthshire, Wales
d: Dec 1885 in Illinois?

Reece Williams
1792 - 1870
b: 1792 in Llangammarch,
Brecknockshire, Wales
d: 28 Feb 1870 in Tremont,
Schuylkill, Pennsylvania, United
States

Ann Williams
1801 - Bet. 1841-1851
b: 1801 in Wales
d: Bet. 1841-1851 in Wales

Ada Hazel Clark
1874 - 1941
b: 16 Apr 1874 in Middletown, NY?
d: 02 Jan 1941 in Battle Creek, MI

James M. Clark
1851 - 1922
b: 29 Jan 1851 in Middletown,
Orange, New York, United States
d: 06 Aug 1922 in Tulsa,
Oklahoma, USA; Rose Hill
Memorial Park

Chauncey H. Clark
1816 - 1883
b: 1816 in Orange Co, NY
d: 01 Feb 1883 in Wawayanda,
Orange Co. NY (Hillside Cem.
Middletown)

Mary C. Corwin
1823 - 1890
b: 11 Sep 1823 in Wallkill, Ulster,
New York, United States
d: 13 May 1890 in Middletown, NY
(3 spring st.)

Cornelia Johnson Snyder
1850 - 1940
b: 12 Jan 1850 in Round Hill,
Greenwich, Connecticut, United
States
d: 07 Feb 1940 in Battle Creek, MI

William D. Snyder
1818 - 1894
b: 1818 in Dutchess Co., NY?
(marriage of Ida)
d: 17 Mar 1894 in Stamford, CT;
Stamford newspaper April 7, 1894

Eliza Jane Brown
1815 - 1900
b: 28 Mar 1815 in Round Hill,
Greenwich, Connecticut, United
States
d: 22 Mar 1900 in Chicago, Cook
Co., IL

Chapter 5

Laura Anne Bell

Laura Anne Bell, was born on Jan 14, 1887 in South Shields, Durham County, England. She was the seventh of eight children born to Joseph Watson Bell and Elizabeth Blumer Purvis. Her dad was a butcher, so Laura learned the meat business at a young age. Among the meat-related stories she would tell were the times she drank warm blood and ate blood pudding. A carving connoisseur, she would capably wield a knife and steel and put on quite a show cutting the ham or turkey.

A young man named John Swainston lived in the same area of South Shields as Laura. As young adults, the two of them took an interest in each other. While Laura stayed home working at her father's butchers' shop, John traveled the world but ended up settling in New York City. During four years of living in New York City, John would make biannual visits to England to see his family and, more importantly, Laura. Because of the distance between them, the two of them would go for long periods of time without seeing each other. To Laura, it felt like eons. After one of John's biannual visits to England to see her, Laura finally had had enough. She was determined to make their love work. She made up her mind to leave the familiar confines of South Shields and left on the long voyage across the Atlantic, heading for the unknown adventure that was the Big Apple. John had family in the U.S., but Laura was the first, and possibly only one in her family, to leave England. The risky move paid off as she soon married John. The day after she arrived in New York they were married.

Laura's first two daughters, Elizabeth and Laura, were born in NYC. Her son Donald was born in Battle Creek, Michigan where the Swainstons moved, after

Laura had been in NYC for three years. When Laura was 39, she learned she was expecting the couple's 4th child.

Those early years in Battle Creek were a struggle. The family struggled financially. Finances were the least of their struggles. Their son Donald had tuberculosis. Even worse, he could not walk because he had been run over by a car in the driveway. Laura feared another child would just add to their woes. Laura, her daughter, once stated that she could sense that her mother did not really want another child. In fact, the family reported that Laura would eat many beets as it was an old wive's tale that eating beets could cause a miscarriage. On Sept 9th a baby girl was born to Laura. Sadly, the child was stillborn. Laura had no relatives in the states. They all remained in England. Her daughters remember that she had an, unknown to them, uncle back in England that used to send her expensive gifts, which the family sold to assist their income.

More than anything, Laura wanted to see her son Donald healed. At one point she took him in a wagon to a church having healing services. Incredibly, Donald was healed. He went on to excel in school. Laura was often quoted as saying, "We might be poor, but we don't have to look poor." Consequently, everyone in the family dressed well. Eugene Keathley remembers his classmate, Donald Swainston wearing a suit every day at Battle Creek Central high school.

After John started selling real estate, Laura soon followed. John then returned to painting houses. Laura was not only a real estate salesperson, but she was also a real estate broker. She never sold more than three or four houses a year. They never had a steady income.

Raising two girls is difficult, especially when they reach those early teen years. Laura, the daughter, was 13 years old when she met and began dating an older man, Robert (Bob) Harris, age 19. To add to John and Laura's concern for their daughters, shortly after this their daughter Elizabeth, age 15, started dating Robert's *older* brother George Harris. Elizabeth's parents did not approve of the union, so she waited until she was 21 to marry George. Bob married Laura when she was 20. We don't know why Grandma Laura never approved of George and Elizabeth. She did not seem to have a problem with Robert and Laura. We were never sure of the reason.

For a short time, George and Elizabeth, after they had their first two boys, lived in the same house as John and Laura. Elizabeth and George had five boys. They never had any girls. Elizabeth could never understand why her parents didn't like her dating an older boy. Today, it is unthinkable for a young girl in the 9th grade to date a boy one or two years out of high school or a boy who never graduated. This would be difficult for any parent.

Laura's woes would continue. Her son Donald, then a 24-year-old senior at Western Michigan University, died unexpectedly. Laura was then 57 years old. Two years later, her daughter Laura became mentally ill after the birth of her only daughter, Becky. Laura, the daughter, would be in and out of mental institutions for the next 30 years. Grandma Laura and John felt it best if their daughter Laura lived at home with them, outside the hospital environment. Grandma cared for her daughter from then on except for the few times she was hospitalized. Their daughter Laura had electric shock treatments to treat her mental illness on seven occasions.

Laura and John and their daughter Laura Harris would frequent the George Harris farm for birthdays, Christmas, Thanksgiving, and summer picnics. Roast beef and Yorkshire pudding were often served as an English tradition. Her recipe has been handed down to Elizabeth and her children and grandchildren. Every year, Grandma Laura would make an English Christmas Pudding with rum sauce. We have since lost the recipe, but we remember it had suet in the recipe. Laura usually gave the prayer before family meals. She always added prayer for salvation for her grandsons George or Jim. I don't think they appreciated the spotlight.

The grandchildren remember that in their home in Battle Creek, they always had orange candy slices on the coffee table, it was usually just one piece each. Grandma Laura introduced the family to a delicacy, that is Vernors ginger ale.

In scanning through the Battle Creek Newspapers, we find very interesting articles that involve Laura. In March 1950, The Enquirer and News published a large article titled "Many Local Women Following Careers in the Real Estate Field". Laura was 63 at that time. While the article mentioned several Women in real estate one half of the article was devoted to Laura, with a two-column wide photo of her on the telephone. They referred to her as the "Dean of Women Brokers", with 30 years in the business. The article stated that Laura helped her father, a butcher, in South Shields, England manage his property for 15 years before she came to New York. She passed her state board examination in 1920. In March of 1950 another article appeared in the Enquirer and News. This article titled "Woman, 77, Holds Bible and Orders Holdup Man Out". This article describes a situation where a man came to the front door with a gun and demanded money. Laura, always the woman of faith, stepped back, picked up her Bible and pointed it at the man saying, "In the name of Jesus Christ leave". "He just left", Mrs. Swainston said. They were members of the Calvary Baptist Church.

Laura died in her sleep, the night of August 6, 1969, at the age of 72. Grandpa John woke up in the morning and Laura did not respond, so he called their daughter Elizabeth. Laura, John and son Donald are buried in the same plot at Memorial Park cemetery in Battle Creek, Michigan.

There are two things we can all take from the life of Laura Anne Bell Swainston. First, you can be poor, but you do not have to look poor. Second, if you have grandchildren, provide something around the house that they can remember you by: Orange slices, Vernors, Eskimo pies, root beer floats, ice cream malts, chips, or jellybeans. The simple things make life a little more special.

Chapter 6

John Simpson Swainston

On June 12, 1884, John Simpson Swainston was born in South Shields (Durham) on the Northeastern shore of England, to Richard Swainston and Mary Jane Simpson. John was born into a family of sailors as John's father, uncles, and many cousins were sailors. When John was ten years old, his mother died after the birth of his younger sister Ida. John's father remarried. From this new union John had two stepsiblings, Richard and Frances Mary.

When John was 17, he signed on as an "Ordinary Apprentice's Indenture". This led him around the world for the next four years. Young John, being only 17 years old, had to have his stepmother, Frances, sign for him to enter his indentured service. For his servitude he was paid 6 pounds for his first year, 8 pounds for his second year, 10 pounds for his third year, and 16 pounds for his fourth year of service. John's apprenticeship ended one month after his 21st birthday, in beautiful Rio de Janeiro. He signed on to another ship to get himself back to South Shields. In 2024 dollars, he averaged about $2000 a year. With a taste for adventure, the following year John visited New York City. This time he traveled as a passenger and not a sailor. He would return to New York every two years. Once at age 24, again at age 26, and for the final time in 1914 at age 28. This time he decided to stay. He took up permanent residence in New York City and found employment at a magazine printing company. Legend has it that on these earlier trips to the United States, the adventurous John would hop on freight trains and make his way to California and back.

Between his New York and South Shields travels, John spent enough time in South Shields to meet a girl three years younger than him, one Laura Anne Bell. Laura lived in the same community of Westoe. They decided they would marry. John would return to England for a visit in early 1914. In March of that year John returned to his work and home in NYC. He and Laura must have made some important plans in that short visit, because three months later Laura followed John

31

to The Big Apple. They wasted no time, and they were married as soon as she arrived. By now John was a more mature 30 and Laura was 27.

The honeymooners wasted no time starting their family as their daughter Ida Elizabeth joined them just over nine months later. A second daughter, Laura Anne, arrived two years later. Three years in NYC was enough. John and Laura moved their young family to Battle Creek, Michigan, where John had an aunt Annie (Swainston) Allan, and an Uncle Thomas Swainston. Two years after this move to the Midwest, their son Donald John was born. By this time, John was working as a painter.

As the Great Depression was waning, John, now age 49, was selling real estate to supplement his income as a house painter. Later in life, the Swainstons found that Laura was better in real estate than was John. John acted as her driver while Laura did the selling. The Swainstons always struggled financially, never owning their own home. Instead, they would struggle to pay their rent and often moved from one rental house location to the next, staying one step ahead of the landlord.

The family remembers that one time John, then in his late 70s, painted the family Chevrolet II a light blue color using only a paint brush. While John did not drink, there were occasions when his grandson George would slip him a beer. John would sip on that beer. We were not sure if he liked the beer or the connection it gave him with George.

John passed away just three months after losing his wife of 54 years. After her death, he was disoriented and spent his last three months in a nursing home in Marshall, Michigan. He is buried in his family plot at Memorial Park, in Battle Creek.

Closest living relatives through John's line: Lyndon Swainston and Patricia Swainston Watson. Lyndon lives in London, England and Patricia, her sister lives in Cardiff, Wales. They are two cousins on their father's side to David Harris. They are also second cousins once removed on their mother's side. John's younger sister was Ida Swainston. Her son was Raymond Cox Swainston, the father of these two girls.

The next closest relative would be Matthew Allen (3rd cousin) who still lives in Battle Creek. His grandfather was Thomas Richard Allan. Thomas was John Swainston's cousin. There are many other descendants of Thomas Allan living today (17 grandchildren).

Chapter 7

Laura Anne Swainston

Laura Anne Swainston, was born in New York General Hospital on August 20, 1916, in Bronx, New York. Her father was John Simpson Swainston and mother, Laura Annie Bell. Her parents had come to the US from South Shields, England prior to 1914. Laura's family of four including her sister Ida Elizabeth moved to Battle Creek, Michigan when she was just one year old. She had no extended family in New York. All her grandparents, aunts, uncles and cousins were all living in England. The move to Battle Creek allowed her to grow up with her father's extended family.

Her father became a house painter once they were in Battle Creek. Because the economy was weak, her mother began selling real estate. She was quite successful. December 16, 1919, Laura's brother Donald John was born. The family lived comfortably until the mid 1920s when Donald fell out of an automobile, hitting his spine on a curb leaving him paralyzed from the waist down. They lost their house because of medical expenses and were forced to move many times due to a lack of rent money.

At age 13, Laura met Robert (Bob) Holbrook Harris (19) at a church youth group Halloween party. After that meeting, they spent time at church and going to movies. It was the depression, so it was a difficult time in the world. Laura graduated from Battle Creek Central High School in 1935. Bob paid for her to attend secretarial school after that. She had two secretarial jobs before becoming an executive secretary for an advertising vice president at Kellogg Company. In her free time, she enjoyed drawing, table tennis and trips to Lake Michigan.

Laura and Bob finally married August 28, 1939, at the First Methodist church. They went to Niagara Falls and New York City on their honeymoon. Part of that time was spent at the World's Fair in Flushing, NY and watching ocean liners on the Hudson River. One of them was the Bremen from Germany. It sailed out and never returned as World War II began before it reached Germany.

Laura continued to work at Kellogg Co. and Bob at Clark Equipment Co, however he was transferred to the Buchanan, MI plant for a year and a half because of the war. He

Figure 6. Laura and Bob

commuted weekly while Laura remained at home. After Pearl Harbor, Bob returned to Battle Creek and worked twelve-hour days. They were in a group of six couples that partied on weekends to alleviate the stress of the war. Just prior to the end of the war, this group of couples reorganized the YMCA and YWCA in Battle Creek. It had been out of business for over twenty years.

Figure 7. Laura with Becky

When Laura was 29, she quit her job at Kellogg's. Their daughter, Becky Sue Harris was born October 16, 1945. The next year they moved into a house on 357 Edna Street. Laura spent her time caring for Becky, their home and with neighborhood friends. In 1948 the wife of the next-door neighbor became mentally ill. This effected Laura considerably as they were close. For whatever reason, Laura had a mental breakdown shortly after that friend moved away. She was taken to the local hospital where her disease deteriorated. She was diagnosed with schizophrenia. It was determined the only facility that could help her was the State Mental Hospital in Kalamazoo. While there she received electric shock therapy. She remained there two or three years until her mother had her discharged without Bob's consent. He was having difficulties paying for her stay there and had difficulties at work because of what was going on. Becky was staying with Elizabeth's family. Bob was living at home and would visit both on weekends. He eventually moved to Elizabeth's and rented his home to save money

Laura lived with her parents after leaving the State Hospital. She was not cured but her mother wanted to care for her. It was a difficult situation as Laura was generally catatonic but could become hostile, although not violent. Bob divorced Laura five years after her illness began. He had hoped the shock of the divorce would cause Laura to want to come home to him. When that didn't happen, he and Becky left Elizabeth's to live at their home on Edna St. Her parents continued to care for Laura and seek medical treatment. It would occasionally be necessary to return to the hospital for short term treatment. Psychotic medications were being developed that helped somewhat.

As her parents aged, Laura was placed in foster care. She lived in a home in Urbandale with five or six others. The new drugs were helping. After her parents died in 1969, Laura became an Incapacitated Ward of the State. Her life was managed by an appointed guardian and her caregivers. Becky was married and moved to Milwaukee in 1970. Her sister was busy with her family. Eventually Laura moved to another foster home on Cherry Street. While there, another new drug was introduced that helped even more. The foster home caregivers were very good to Laura and even took her to Florida on vacation. In February 1983, Laura was able to be released from the court guardianship and became independent.

Laura enjoyed being independent. She managed her home, expenses & medications, used public transportation, dressed well, and participated in activities at home and at church. Laura enjoyed drawing with watercolors and colored pencils, bingo and reading. She drew and sent Christmas and birthday cards to her favorite people. This included her two grandchildren in Milwaukee. She was always happy when they came to visit. In the early 1990s, Laura resumed a friendship with Dorothy Flanders Orwig. Dorthy had been one of the groups that revived the YMCA, but also a medical social worker. Dorothy helped Laura move into her own independent senior living apartment in Urbandale. A highlight for Laura was attending her grandson's wedding in 1994.

Laura fell in August 2003 just before her 87th birthday. She had been hit by a bicycle in 1994 and had a hip replacement. Because of this and her age, the doctors would not do another surgery. She went into a nursing home then and was active for a while but eventually began to fail. Laura died December 10, 2003, at the age of 87. She is buried in the Memorial Park cemetery in the plot owned by Robert Harris. Compiled by Becky Kunkler (Harris).

Chapter 8

Donald John Swainston

In the bustling town of Battle Creek, Michigan in December 1919, Donald John Swainston entered the world, the youngest son of John Simpson Swainston and Laura Annie Swainston. He joined two older sisters, Ida Elizabeth, who had seen four winters, and Laura Ann, three years his senior. The Swainston home, though modest, was filled with the usual joys and trials of a growing family.

However, fate dealt a cruel blow in 1926. Young Donald, barely seven, suffered a devastating fall from an automobile, his spine striking the unforgiving curb. The impact left him paralyzed from the waist down, a tragedy that would forever alter the course of his life. Doctors, in a desperate attempt to restore his mobility, operated on his back to remove bone fragments, but the remedy proved incomplete.

The financial burden of Donald's medical care proved insurmountable. The Swainston family, already struggling, lost their home, forced to wander from one rented dwelling to another, their lives a constant search for affordable shelter. Amidst these hardships, his mother, Laura Annie, a woman of deep and unwavering faith, sought solace and healing. One day, she took Donald to a church where a faith healer was said to perform miracles. Donald, carried in on a wagon, emerged walking, a testament to his mother's belief. Despite his physical limitations, Donald's spirit remained unbroken. He excelled in his studies, graduating high school with honors. A classmate remembered him as a young man of dignity, always impeccably dressed in a suit, a reflection of his mother's insistence that even in poverty, one could maintain an outward appearance of respect.

His academic achievements earned him a scholarship to Western Michigan University, where he continued to shine. He served as Treasurer of the student government during his junior year, demonstrating a keen mind and a talent for leadership. To support himself, he worked part-time at a shoe store and as a draftsman at Post Cereal Co., proving his determination and resourcefulness.

It was at university that Donald found love, a young woman who captured his heart. However, their budding romance was met with disapproval from his mother, who seemed to disapprove of the young woman and her lifestyle. Whatever the reasons, the relationship was tragically cut short.

During his senior year, Donald's health took a devastating turn. He was diagnosed with tuberculosis of the kidneys, an incurable disease in that era. He returned home to his parents, where he spent his final days. On January 14, 1944, at the tender age of 24, Donald John Swainston passed away. He was laid to rest in Memorial Park Cemetery beside his beloved parents.

Chapter 9

Robert Holbrook Harris

<u>There Were To Squirrels</u>
<u>That Lived in the Woods</u>

An Autobiography, written for my Grand-nephew, Mark Harris, in appreciation for his efforts in tracing our family genealogy, from Robert Harris.

Yes Mark, I was born to parents as are all living things. Even as an acorn is born from an oak tree and the stork bears baby storks and not baby humans. The two squirrels that live in the woods thou they were probably real squirrels were to me a product of fantasy, for I learned about them from the first poem that was taught to me.

My parents told me that I was born to them in the suburb of Chicago, a place called Downers Grove. The year was 1911. Of this I do not doubt for there is a birth certificate (of which I have a copy) on record in that county. There is also a certificate showing my mother enrolled me in the cradle roll of the church they attended near their home.

My parents moved from that little suburb when I was still a small baby, and I do not recollect whether they asked if it was ok with me. You know how parents are when they want to move and are in a hurry to get to another place. My dad was offered a job with a railroad, the town was away from the big city of Chicago, a place where we grow not among buildings made by man of cement and steel but a place where there were trees and grass aplenty for two small boys. A place where they could watch and laugh at the antics of those two squirrels that lived in the wood and have as much freedom to play and work.

Now comes the time in my life when I begin to remember things that happened and there are a few things I would like to forget. I would like to forget the little hurts my parents suffered just because of my careless and mischievous behavior, they that is part of growing up. As I remember they got their licks in as they said, "This is going to hurt me more than it hurts you."

School as usual started in the kindergarten, which was time spent coloring, making ABC's and playing games. Those ABCs were "old hat" to me because my Great-Aunt Florence (who was a teacher) had taught those symbols and numerals to me She had taught me so well that I skipped the first grade and went to second the following year.

Now school was fun, but it was more fun to stop at Number three fire station on the way home and pet the fire horses. In those days we did not have fire engines with gasoline engines like we have today. The firemen lived part time at the fire station and when there was a fire, they slid down a pole from their upstairs room and hitched the horses to the steamer (that was the piece of equipment they used to make pressure to squirt the water) and to the ladder wagon. It was a thrill for a small boy and even grown-ups to watch them go. When they came back, at times, the firemen would give me a handful of hay to feed the horses. That's when I wanted to be a fireman.

At home we had plenty of time to laugh and play and before it was dark, we were in bed although there were times my brother, George (who is your grandfather) and I would not calm down until our dad came in with his razor strap. Now parents use paddles and at times switches to enforce their rules on the likes of children who are overly noisy and misbehave, but there is no instrument to quiet a small boy like a razor strap. Our dad just had to make a noise by hitting it on his hand and under the covers we would go. Not to be heard of till next day.

We did not have an automobile at that time, those came later. We had street cars that went past the house. And tall Mr. Lowe with his short wife. Mr. Lowe was a machinist and worked at the railroad shops with my dad. There was the little girl who lived across the street and was a playmate, and there was the boy who lived next door where I went to my first party. My grandmother asked me when I returned home if I had remembered to say "Yes, if you please and no thank you" when asked. My reply was, I said "Yes if you please but not no thank you", because I wanted some of everything. Soon after this we moved to another house.

The new house was larger than the one we had lived in. My two great aunts had come from the east (Connecticut) to live with us, and we had to have more room. My brother and I had our room in the attic on the third floor at first. Later we were given the bedroom on that floor, and it seemed miles from the rest of the family. Outside our bedroom window was a large oak tree and there is where I spent time learning the ways of the little black and red squirrels as they gathered acorns.

Whole new worlds opened to us in our new home. New playmates, a different school, new games, a garden to help work, above all a chance to plant and watch things grow. Mark: that is the finer things in life to me, to watch change, to see and to accept the difference, and to know that we can do things with our time that will be of help to ourselves and others. My brother and I found plenty of time for learning new ways. Weeding carrots and washing windows were things that had to be done for it was a custom of the adults to look out the windows (as I also learned to do) and the carrots were tasty when one played and worked.

We did our schoolwork when we got home from school and then we changed our clothes to go out to play. Our dad could place a finger and thumb in his mouth and whistle loud enough to be heard at least two blocks away, this was a signal that supper was on the table. After supper we were allowed to go play until dark. There were three to do the dishes, so we seldom did that chore. Dad usually spent time in the garden after supper in the summertime and early fall

Games early in our lives were Run Sheep Run, Tag, Red light, Duck on the Rock, May I, Statues. We made scooters out of a roller skate, a two by four and a soap box. We made our own kites out of sticks, newspaper and paste and spent many enjoyable hours flying them. We climbed the trees in the apple orchard back of our house and one time acquired the wrath of the neighbors when we set the grass on fire. Halloween was a time we could let loose and do things we could not do any other times of the Year.

Halloween was a time for differences if ever there was a time. It was a time where we could make the differences and changes. Porch furniture was hung on telephone poles, outhouses were tipped over, streetcar trolleys were tripped and the tracks greased so the wheels spun, in smaller towns' buggies that were horse drawn and wagons were disassembled and reassembled on the roof of barns. What one of us could not think of, another could, much to the chagrin of the adults. Don't tell your dad I told you this.

When I was nine or ten years of age, I earned money selling the magazines Saturday Evening Post, Country Gentlemen, and Ladies Home Journal. The first two sold for a nickel and the other a dime. We did not become millionaires. My buddy had a newspaper route, and it later became mine. It started in the downtown area and ended up on the other side of the cemetery from our home. As the days grew darker in the evening it was sometimes necessary that I would walk around the outside stone wall rather than cutting thru the center. I wasn't scared just not courageous to tangle with spooks. Later my brother and I delivered papers close to home. We had a route of over four hundred papers to carry.

World War I was over. During those years we acquired our first automobile. It was a two-family affair. It was a seven passenger Chandler and there were ten of us in the two families. My uncle Willis drove, and his favorite saying was, "look your eyes out kids, this is costing us money." The first trip I remember had a detour where we went thru a farmer's field to get from one country road to another. It was in the spring of the year and cars were up to their axles in mud (not moving). Somehow, we got out without getting stuck and we did not get to where we wanted to go.

Later we went to Lake Michigan, and it was an all-day trip. An early start and home by dark. A few times we stayed overnight. There was a big amusement park by the lake which is now gone. Benton Harbor was larger than its twin, St Joe. Passenger boats came there from Chicago though we never rode across the lake on them, it looked like a challenge. A short time later my dad bought his own automobile, a Dodge Touring car with special eisenglass windows to keep out the rain and cold and plenty of room for six people. We were in seventh heaven so to speak.

The year nineteen twenty-three marked the beginning of a new era in my life for it was then I joined the Boy Scouts. New friends, new challenges, no television, it was years in the future. Radio for our family was a crystal set with a telephone receiver that my brother acquired from somewhere by trading something. Hearing KDKA station in Pittsburg was a marvel of science to us at that time. Back to Scouting, new recruits made a hike out west of town about four miles. Here the officers had spent the morning digging fire pits and were cooking beef in chunks. It was my first "Ox-roast". We were introduced to a new game called Capture the Flag. The Blues were on the north side of the creek and the Reds on the South (We wore armbands of those colors). The object of the game, to capture a flag the opponents had placed in their territory and return to our side without getting caught by one of their players. They had to do likewise without being caught by one of our players. Many fell in the creek, but the fun and the feed of Ox sandwiches hooked me on Scouting.

I shall return later to the topic of scouting because of the effect scouting had on my life. For now, let us turn our thoughts to other things. Circus and parades; everyone loves a parade. When the circus came to town it was for one day. We were up at the crack of dawn to watch the unloading from the railroad cars. The wagons were pulled up the street past our house by teams of horses and sometimes by elephants to the circus ground which was about three blocks away. Later the wagons and animals were assembled to parade down thru town. We sat on our front lawn or the curb to watch them go past and return. My first job with the circus was "watering the elephants" which means carrying pails of water to them to drink and spray on themselves and others. Later as I grew older it was putting up the tents, the side show and the "big top", also erecting the seats. For this we earned a ticket to the show which I went to in the afternoon. I learned early that to pick up the pop bottles after the show one could earn another ticket for the evening performance. By doing these little jobs I learned more how to work and to love and respect those animals that came from faraway places.

During these times school managed to keep us going and we had about one mile to walk. Second, third, and fourth grade we stayed in the same room for the day. Twice a day was recess and time for play. Dodge ball was my fun game for it was not much fun to get one's shins kicked while playing soccer. Baseball was ok if the girls would not throw their bat. Fifth grade we went into departmental. Now we went to six different rooms with six different teachers, and six special subjects: Penmanship, the Palmer method, fractions, English, geography, music. My parents bought me a violin which they had to put up with for about two years. I later traded it for a chromatic harmonica which I still have. Fifth grade, and my first real girlfriend. She moved away during the year and it near broke my heart for she did not say good-bye or say just where she was going.

In the year nineteen twenty-four or five. We often hiked down by the river and across the river; a golf course was built (now Riverside). "Kid, do you want to learn to caddy": and I was sold on golf. My cousin (Raymond) and I were caddies. We earned seventy-five cents by carrying clubs for the distance of eighteen holes. Most days we carried in the morning and later in the afternoon. With a tip we took home two dollars. At times when dew was on the ground, we were given fish (cane) poles to get the water off the greens. For this effort we were allowed to play on the golf course on Monday morning and some days the pro would watch and give us lessons. My cousin and I owned one club each, a mid-iron, which we used for all shots. I saved enough money in the spring to pay my way to scout camp. (First round of golf at age 13)

In Junior high, grades eight and nine. Now we walked twice as far to school. Some of our old schoolmates and many new ones from all parts of the city. My school marks were not the best, but I managed to pass to a higher level each term. Scouting was one reason perhaps for lack of school study. There was much to do and many new things to learn. Every new merit badge was another challenge, and I earned fifty-six of them (only 26 required for Eagle Scout) which means that many new branches to my tree of education were added. It led to summer work at camp counseling younger boys, Eagle tours to faraway places, one of which was the bush country in Ontario where we learned to canoe white water, observe moose, bear, loons, catch trout, and hear the wolves howl as we lay in sleeping bags on a bed made of pine boughs. Today at most three score and ten it is still a desire to go each year and rekindle those moments, to sit by an open fire with friends, watch the stars, moon, clouds and the northern lights when they seem to dance in the sky.

The late twenties. Four years of high school. Higher levels of mathematics, English, history, science (chemistry and physics) woodworking, mechanical drawing, literature, economics, etc. all led to the challenges that were to come later. It was not always "do as I say" by our teachers, we learned to ask questions for there are times the books do not have the best answers. To me a teacher who follows a book verbatim is not the best one to teach. We have to keep testing the things we have learned with the observations we see each moment of the day. Many times, our direction is changed by following what our nose, or ear, or eye, etc. seem to say. Aristotle was a very learned man in his day, but he made a drastic mistake by observing and inferring that the world was flat. Today we know different, (and it is not truly round either). Maybe someday some will find the secret of, "How far is up". You could be that one, but do not dwell on that problem too long. It is a toughie, and you may miss many other things in this universe.

Other occupations; Included clerking and delivering groceries. Working in a feed and grain mill. Serving food and washing dishes in a cafeteria. Mowing lawns. Selling house to house. Cleaning houses for invalid people. Working with a survey team. Clerking in a clothing store and even driving rich dowagers to and from with the use of their Cadillac's.

This brings me up to graduation from high school. The year was nineteen twenty-nine. The same year of the stock market crash and economic depression. Jobs were hard to find even for those who had much talent. Students whose parents had money safely put away could go on to college. Others including me and some of my friends would sometimes find a job for a day. Sweeping the floor, dusting machines of sawdust and wood chips in a pattern shop was worth one dollar for a Saturday morning. A job in a drafting department at twenty-five cents an hour only lasted a short time, but it was a step for other things to come.

The time, approximately twenty years, was consumed in doing the above things mentioned. There were no great things accomplished to change the destiny of the work, just little things that any person could have done, and many people did things similar. Fly kites, water elephants or just walk in the rain. Some of these you too can do if you take the time. Time to observe, change, adjust to change and differences, and as the late Walter Hagen once said, "Take time to smell the flowers along the way"

Your Uncle Bob

Robert H. Harris
August 14, 1979

Robert Holbrook Harris was born on June 4, 1911, in Downers Grove, Illinois. We affectionately called him Uncle Bob, and he wrote an autobiography covering his first twenty years. I will attempt to recount the remaining eighty years of his life.

At the age of 20, Bob and his brother George, who was 21, attended a dance at the YWCA. It was there that Bob met a much younger girl named Laura Swainston. Bob was two years out of high school, while Laura was just entering her sophomore year. They began dating, and since the boys had the family car, it made it convenient for double dates; later, George would date a girl named Elizabeth who was Laura's older sister, had a similar age difference.

With the drafting skills he learned in high school, Bob found a career as a draftsman with Clark Equipment Co. in Battle Creek. He started as a tracer or layout draftsman and eventually progressed to become the head of the tool design department. A few years after his marriage, he moved to Buchanan, Michigan, with Clark Equipment, but he eventually returned to Battle Creek.

Bob Dated Laura for seven years and they were married when he was 27 and Laura was 21.

It would be another seven years after marriage before their only child, Becky, was born. Sometime before Becky's birth, Laura began to have a mental illness problem. That same year Laura was declared mentally insane by the courts. Now, the tough years began. How do you care for a newborn and raise her while your wife is insane? Bob and Laura would divorce, and Bob would raise Becky. Laura would live with her parents and spend many unsuccessful stays in the mental institution in Kalamazoo. We referred it as the "Third Hill in Kalamazoo."

For a couple years when Becky was starting school, Bob and Becky moved in with George and Elizabeth on their farm- with four boys and Grandpa Joe.

When Becky was in high school, Bob remarried Velma Spencer. Velma had three children of her own, and two were still living at home. That marriage lasted less than two years as Velma died from a medication interaction. This now left Bob with Becky, Phil, and Denny.

I recall on the farm we had some snow skis that John and I used. They were nothing compared to skis today. You slid your boot into it. Also, a leather military pilot's hat- which was very warm in the winter snow. They were hand-me-downs from Bob's earlier years.

Working at Clark equipment, many of Bob's coworkers, especially in engineering, had their boys in the Soap Box Derby. Bob did not have boys, but he had nephews and I (David) wanted to be in the soap box derby. Bob was able to get used wheels and axles for me. On two occasions Bob took me to a wood saw mill and purchased a 2 ½ inch thick oak plank to use as a base for the cars. This is when I first had a salami sandwich on Rye bread with mustard as he fixed lunch at his house.

I remember Bob had a bumper pool table in his basement which we used many times. One year Bob gave us (boys) a knock hockey board which was a lot like air hockey before they had the air. We spent many hours playing with it on the dining room table on the farm.

Bob liked to travel, and he owned several travel trailers over the years. He also had a small motor home. His favorite was the Airstream travel trailer.
Bob's third wife was Greta, and they had many happy years together.

Bob's favorite sport was Golf. His best friend in high school became a club pro in Florida. His last round of golf was played at the age of 100, which gave him 87 years of playing golf. He never hit a hole-in-one but when he moved to Milwaukee and was done playing golf, we found a shoe box of golf balls all marked with different distances. These were hole-in-ones he got in his small side-yard golf hole. He didn't count those as real hole-in-ones.

Figure 8. Bob Harris on his 100th birthday

Bob was also an avid fisherman starting with his boy scout years. Bob owned a cabin in Canada where he would go to fish. When Bob was over 80 years old, he would take trips to the Baha Peninsula of Mexico with his nephew George. They would deep sea fish for a week, staying in a small fishing village.

Chapter 10

Joseph Harris
(1875 - 1966)

Joseph Harris was born on March 5, 1875, in Wiconisco, Dauphin Co., PA, which is about ten miles east of Tremont. He was the youngest of ten children born to Joseph and Lenah Harris, both of whom were born in Wales. According to their family Bible, Joseph's nine siblings were all born in Tremont, PA. In those days, there were no birth certificates, and the only documentation of Joseph's birth is the family, Bible. Because he had no birth certificate, when Joseph went to retire in 1940, he established his age by using this family Bible, and the testimony of a relative and a schoolmate from Braceville, IL.

Right before Joseph's birth, the country was in the midst of its first depression. The Harris family, in search of better coal mining jobs, moved from Tremont, PA to the nearby town of Wiconisco/Lykens, PA. By 1877, when Joseph was two years old, the Harris family lived in Lykens, Pennsylvania when it experienced what has been infamously called "the year in hell." Tragically, a fire started in the coal mines and burned for an entire year creating extreme poverty and suffering. Sometime before 1880, the Harris family moved to Mansfield, Pennsylvania, located about five miles south of Pittsburg, PA. The 1880 census showed that Joseph, now five years old, his parents, and all his siblings lived there.

By his own testimony, Joseph only attended school through the fifth grade. Interestingly, it is noted in his fifth grade McGuffey reader that Joseph and most of the rest of his immediate family now lived in Braceville, IL with his grandparents and his aunts and uncles. Jemima his older sister stayed in Pittsburgh, PA where she married. After Braceville Joseph lived with his oldest brother John in Spring Valley, Illinois, for a short time. From census records we know that when he was 25, he was living with his sister Lydia and her husband Marvin Bates in Chicago.

When Joseph was 18 one of his highlights was attending the "World Columbian Exposition". Held every four years, in different countries and cities, they would showcase new products and displays from around the world. The 1893 expo, in Chicago was to celebrate the 400th anniversary of Columbus' discovery of America. Grandpa kept memorabilia from this "World's Fair", on his desk. That fair which was a year late had a Venetian theme as they built a moat around all the buildings and navigated the water from Lake Michigan in gondolas.

When Joseph was 22 the news was "there was gold in the Yukon". Joseph had two brothers who were still gold miners. He had two minor friends who had planned for the three of them to head for the Yukon and stake their claim. Fortunately for his future family, his two friends backed out.

According to family lore, Joseph was quite the athlete. He would ride cross-country bicycle races in Northern Illinois. He played softball with an extra large 16" ball. He would hit the ball straight down at the ground, so the ball would bounce high in the air. Using this technique, Joseph could always beat out the throw to first base.

Joseph worked for the railroads by investigating lost and stolen products from railcars. In one grand find, he once found a missing boxcar full of Remington guns. While necessary, Joseph often did not enjoy wearing his own .38 pistol.

Then, love struck. 34-year-old Joseph met a sweet young lady named Ada Hazel Clark. Joseph and Ada, who was six years his junior, married on April 9, 1909. Upon closer inspection of school records and early census records, we learn that Ada was actually two years older than Joseph. We don't know the cause of this discrepancy. Was it Ada's little secret? We will never know; we can only speculate. But, in the end, it doesn't really matter, as love is love. The newlyweds started their married lives, with Ada's mother Cornelia on Garfield Avenue in Chicago.

Joseph and Ada had two sons. The oldest, George, was born in 1910 and in 1912, Robert soon followed. Willis Mitchell, Joseph's brother-in-law, moved to Battle Creek, MI. Joseph, Ada, and the young boys followed him to Battle Creek around 1914. Joseph transferred his job from Chicago to Battle Creek. Joseph and Ada did not own a home but rented a two and a half story home on Main Street. The occupants of that home included Joseph, Ada, George, Robert, Ada's mother Cornelia (until 1939), and Ada's aunts Wilhelmina Snyder (until her death in 1917) and Florence Gray (until 1935).

George and Robert grew up in that home on Main Street. This home was strategically located as Joseph could walk ¼ mile to work daily. Joseph kept a garden in the backyard. For fun, he would often take the interurban train three miles south and rent a boat on Beadle Lake where he liked to fish.

Wilhelmina, upon her death, bequeathed money to both Ada and her sister Elizabeth (Mitchell). The two families combined these funds to purchase the family's first car, a 1917 Chandler. Later Joseph would purchase a Dodge from around 1923. Joseph began driving at age 45 and decided to stop driving at age 65 because of a car accident. About the time he gave up his keys, Joseph moved in with George and Elizabeth, who by then had two of their five boys. In the summer of 1947, George and Elizabeth purchased a farmhouse at 11097 Verona Rd. Battle Creek, MI. Joseph, known as Grandpa Joe, lived in a small upstairs bedroom. He retired from the Grand Trunk Railroad and received a pension of $90 a month. He helped the growing family by contributing $60 a month for his room and board. His $60 paid the home's mortgage for nearly 20 years. Joseph had a hernia and didn't want surgery. Instead, he wore an appliance, a brace. He died in the hospital on June 25, 1966, from complications of prostate surgery.

I am George and Elizabeth's fourth son David. I remember many things about Grandpa Joe. Grandpa Joe was a young, 72-year-old, when I was born. Even when he was in his early 80s, Grandpa Joe was spry. John would run out the house trying to flee punishment, but Grandpa, who was still fleet-of-foot, could catch him before he could get halfway around the house. He usually did the dinner dishes. He would come down in the morning and have two slices of toast and warm his hands around the toaster, because we had no heat upstairs. We had no bathroom upstairs so the young boys would just pee out the window, but Grandpa Joe would use a quart jar, which he discretely brought down every morning. He would walk or hitchhike into Battle Creek once a week. We suspected he was visiting Mable, a female friend. He always wore suspenders. He went to church every Sunday with the youngest boys and Bessie (my mom, Elizabeth). For many years, Grandpa would go to Mount Dora, Florida for a couple months in the winter. He was blessed with free transportation from his railroad retirement and a doctor friend of George's had a spare room in Florida where he could stay.

Grandpa Joe had very few possessions including: a small keyhole desk, an old family Welsh Bible, which he could read, an old McGuffey reader from 5th grade, a single .38 caliber bullet, an autograph book that belonged to his wife, and some pictures. Among the pictures he had was a photo of him with the Reed club at the Chicago Wesleyan Methodist church. He was secretary of the Sunday School there as well. I think two of the members were Kraft brothers of Kraft food fame. One photo was of the Bates Family at a cottage on Lake Geneva, WI, where Grandpa Joe frequently visited on weekends when he lived in Chicago. Other pictures included ones of Ada, himself, Cornelia, Florence and Wilhelmina. Grandpa read Zane Gray books, and he did the newspaper crossword puzzles daily.

I have a theory that could explain a discrepancy in Joseph's genealogy. My theory is that Joseph may be the son of one of his older sisters Jemima or Ann. This is not a joke. I'm saying Joseph's Aunt Jemima may not have been his sister. Several things hint at this.

In 1962, Grandpa Joe, Mom (Elizabeth), Dad (George), my brothers John, Ken, and I went to Walworth, Wisconsin to visit Lenah and Earl Cooper. Grandpa Joe was 10 years older than Lenah. They lived in the same household for many years and by the Bible records Joe would be her uncle. I clearly recall Grandpa and Lenah in a discussion as to their relationship. One thought they were cousins and the other thought the relationship was uncle and niece. They could not agree. It was strange because Grandpa *never* argued. I did not make much of it as I was only sixteen years old and not into genealogy at the time.

The next clue comes from the 1900 census. It shows that Grandpa Joe was in Chicago living with his sister Lydia and her husband Marvin Bates and their four children including Lenah. Living in the same home was Joseph's brother, Isaac T. Curiously, Isaac was correctly listed as a brother-in-law to Marvin while Joseph was listed as a nephew to Marvin.

The obituaries of two of Joseph's siblings Lydia (Harris) Bates and John Harris from Red Lodge, MT do not list Joseph as their sibling.

A **Brick Wall** is a term we use in Genealogy for a problem that could be a dead end - like we can't find the parents of William Snyder. It could be that we have two alternatives to a relationship and neither has the necessary documentation. We keep the Brick wall open until we resolve the issue.

Brick Wall: Who was grandpa Joe's parents? Were they Joseph & Lenah or were they his grandparents?

<u>Known information</u>:

Grandpa Joe* Harris was born on March 5, 1875, in Wiconisco, Dauphin Co., PA, which is about seventeen miles east of Tremont PA in Schuylkill County. He was the youngest of ten children born to Joseph and Lenah Harris, both of whom were born in Wales. Joseph's* nine siblings were all born in Tremont, PA according to census records.

His birth is from the entries in the Joseph & Lenah Harris Welch Family Bible. When he retired from the railroad, he used the Family Bible and letters from School mates to verify his age. There are two sources that support that Joseph and Lenah were his parents, the family Bible and the 1880 census shows him as the son of Joseph and Lenah.

Joseph Harris b. 1826 (Wales) & Lenah Williams b. 1833 (Wales)

1. Ann Harris b. 1855 (no children or spouse known)
2. Jemmima Harris b. 1856 (married Jacob McCormick)
3. John Harris b. 1858 moved to Illinois then Red Lodge, MT.
4. Elizabeth Harris b. 1860 d. 1860 Tremont, PA
5. Isaac T. Harris b. 1862 Married, two children, no grandchild.
6. Lydia Harris b. 1864 d. Chicago 1937 (Elisa in Welch Bible)
7. Joseph Harris b.1866 (d.1872 Tremont, PA)
8. Hannah Harris b. 1869 (d.1872 Tremont, PA)
9. Rees Williams Harris b. 1871 d, 1872 Tremont, PA
10. Joseph* Harris b. 1875 Wiconisco, PA d. 1966 Michigan

Over the years there has been some question of whether Joseph Harris b. 1875 was the child of Joseph and Lenah or possibly the son of either Ann, or Jemmima. Ann would be 19 at Joseph' s conception and Jemmima would be 18. Lenah the mother would be 41 and Joseph 48.

1. The question of who Joseph's (10) parents were started in 1962. I (David Harris), Grandpa Joe, Mom (Elizabeth), Dad (George), my brothers John, and Ken went to Wisconsin to visit Lenah and Earl Cooper. Lenah would be the daughter of Lydia (6) above. I clearly recall Grandpa Joe and Lenah in a heated discussion as to their relationship. One thought they were cousins and the other thought the relationship was aunt and nephew. They could not agree. It was strange because Grandpa *never* argued. I did not make much of it as I was only sixteen years old and not into genealogy at that time.

2. The next clue comes from the 1900 census. It shows that Grandpa Joe was in Chicago living with his sister Lydia (6) and her husband Marvin Bates. Living in the same home was Joseph's brother, Isaac T (5). Curiously, Isaac was correctly listed as a brother-in-law to Marvin while Joseph was listed as a nephew to Marvin. Joseph (10), unlike his siblings, was shown as having parents born in Pennsylvania, not Wales. This supports Lenah's claim that they were cousins not her uncle.

3. The next census, 1910 Grandpa Joe was married to Ada, George was born and living in a completely different household, from the Bates family. That census also showed Joe's parents as being born in Pennsylvania, not Wales. In 1920 Joseph's parents were still shown as born in Pennsylvania. Starting with the 1930 census Joseph's (10) were listed as born in Wales.

4. The obituaries of two of Joseph's* siblings Lydia (6) (Harris) Bates, in Chicago and John (3) Harris from Red Lodge, MT do not list Joseph* as their sibling. Lydia's obituary specifically notes John Harris, Isaac Harris and Mina McCormick as surviving. In John's obituary his only sibling at his death would have been Joseph*. And he was not mentioned.

5. DNA results from three people (23 & me): David Metz (1.74% 130cM), Megan Tiley (.72% 54 cM), and Hugh Jones (.72% 54cM). All three of these are the same or closer than Marvin Bates (Lydia's grandson). They are a 64% chance of being 1/2 2nd cousin or closer. None of these three matches can be found on paper, on my family tree. They all have roots in Centralia, Pa. (a ghost town now) twenty miles north of Tremont and two miles from Ashland. Each if these show up on 23 & me as related, Megan to David 3.21%, Megan to Hugh .81 % and David to Hugh .50%. My mother's (Swainston) side of our family are all from England. My father's mother is from eastern New York and Connecticut. My only possible connection to these three people is through my father's father Joseph Harris (1875). Now the strange thing, if you could go into Megan's, David's or Hugh's, 23 & me account there is no connection to Marvin Bates. If the family tree is correct as published, from the Bible, there should be a similar connection to Marvin by at least one of these three.

If we insert Ann (or Jemmima) as Joseph* Harris's mother and an unknown father, we lose any connection from Marvin Bates to the three Centralia, PA relatives as they would be from the unknown father.

5.Joseph* in the Bible is given the same name as a deceased brother (why another Joseph?). This I have questioned for years.

6.Joseph* The Bible does not show a last name Harris. All other siblings give the last name. He is also listed last and written in another pen.

7. Another problem. The family Bible is usually handed down to the oldest or the child that supports the family unit the most. Ann (1) would be the oldest and Lydia (6) would be the leader of the family. Then how is it that Joseph* ended up with the Bible? Lydia would most likely hand it down to Lenah, her daughter. Perhaps before 1927, when Lydia died, it was passed to Joseph as it would be his only link to the past.

8. As for the 1880 census that showed Joseph as the son of Joseph and Lenah: That census was answered by his brother Issac, and it would be easier to just list Joseph, a 5-year-old, as another member of the family. Also, if Joseph was the son of Jemmima or Ann it would be much more difficult for them to find a spouse to have a child.

Chapter 11

Joseph Harris & Lenah Williams

Joseph Harris Sr. (2) arrived in America 1854 and came directly to Tremont, PA with his wife Lenah Williams. He was 28 and she was 21 and they had no children on arrival. They would have ten children, nine born in Tremont and the last child was born 20 miles west of Tremont in Wiconisco, PA. Four of the children died in Tremont as well as Lenah's father Rees Williams. They lived in Tremont for about 20 years, Wiconisco, PA for about two years, then in what is now Carnegie, PA, for about two years. Their final stop was in Braceville, IL where Joseph's siblings, Solomon, Thomas and Mary were living.

Joseph Harris and Lenah Williams, my great grandparents were born in Wales. They were married May 4th, 1854, in Llanhilleth, Bedwellty, Monmouthshire, Wales. They arrived in Ellis Island / Garden Castle, NYC on Sept 25, 1854. They brought with them a Welch language Bible which is the source of most of our genealogy information.

Lenah was born 17 April 1833 in Llanhilleth, Wales. The death record of a daughter, Lydia Bates states she was born in Swansey, Wales. At some point Lenah Father Reese Williams came to America and lived with them until his death in 1870. He is buried along with three of Lenah's children in the Tremont Methodist Cemetery.

Joseph was born 04 Nov 1826 in Tredegar, Wales. He was the second child of Isaac and Ann Harris. Joseph's older brother Solomon came to America three years earlier. Both boys as well as other family members were coal miners. His parents, Isaac and Ann would come to America later (1863) as Joseph's siblings filtered into the coal mining areas of Pennsylvania.

Solomon and Joseph Sr. settled in the Town of Tremont, PA. They both had enough money to travel to America as well as purchase a home in Tremont. Solomon was the first to leave Tremont, settling in Ohio for a few years then moving to Grundy County Illinois. He was followed by siblings Mary and Thomas and ten years later by Joseph and Lenah. Joseph and Lenah lived in the Tremont, Donaldson area for about 20 years. Joseph, my grandfather, was the youngest of their children, He was born in Wiconisco, PA on March 5, 1875. While Solomon, Mary and Thomas had already moved to Illinois Joseph Sr. had not sold his house in Tremont. The family got caught in the middle of the first great depression now called the panic of 1873. The Panic of 1873 was brought on by high-risk investments into the railroad building business, which occurred following the civil war. Since Joseph owned his home in Tremont he could not just leave and not sell it. Lyken/Wiconisco was about 18 miles west of Tremont and was a good growing mining community. The whole area of central Pennsylvania has Anthracite coal and holds 90% of the world's supply of Anthracite. Anthracite is a hard coal, unlike the more common Bituminous coal. Anthracite burns hotter, slower and cleaner.

Joseph and Lenah were not able to sell their house in Tremont until 1878 when the Harris family could continue moving, headed for family in Illinois. Before the family made that move, they had to endure "A year in Hell" while living in Lyken, PA in 1877. A mine fire in the main mine started on New Year's Day 1877 and burned for an entire year. With no work in the midst of the depression, stealing and looting was common. Google "A year in hell 1877".

Following Joseph and Lenah was not an easy task in the 1870 census their last name was listed as "Karis". This was not hard to find as they were still in Tremont. In the 1880 census their last name was listed as "Teaharris". This took years to find and now shows up on the ancestry websites. The Teaharris most likely stems from one son who had the name Isaac T. Harris and the census taker just wrote "Teaharris."

By 1880 the entire family was still under one roof in Mansfield (now Carnage) PA. south of Pittsburgh. The oldest daughter Ann now 25 and Jemima age 24 were still at home. This would be the last time we find the family all together.

Joseph died in Dec of 1885 and Lenah followed in Nov. 1886 They, along with his parents, Isaac and Ann, are most likely buried in the Cotton Cemetery in Braceville. That cemetery has been overgrown over the years and records have been lost. The only thing left from Joseph and Lenah is the 1854 Welch family Bible. At the time of their deaths Lydia was the only married child living in Illinois. I am assuming she became the caretaker of the Bible. From there it would most likely pass to her daughter, Lenah who was the oldest of her four, but it appears to have passed to her youngest brother Joseph after he married and moved to Michigan. Joseph was living with Lydia in Chicago. From Joseph the Bible passed to his grandson, David.

Descendants of Joseph Harris & Lenah Williams

Name	Birth	Death
Ann	b. March 14, 1855, Tremont, PA	d. Unknown (1935?)
Jemima	b. Nov. 27, 1856, Tremont, PA	d. Oct. 2, 1943, Pittsburgh
John	b. Aug. 12, 1858, Tremont, PA	d. Apr. 21, 1945, MT
Elizabeth	b. May 23, 1860, Tremont, PA	d. 1860 Tremont, PA
Issac T.	b. June 9, 1862, Tremont, PA	d. Apr. 28 1934, Chicago, IL
Lydia	b. June 18, 1864, Tremont, PA	d. Apr. 29 1927, Chicago, IL
Joseph	b. May 25, 1866, Tremont, PA	d. 1872, Tremont, PA
Hanna	b. Nov. 11, 1869, Tremont, PA	d. 1872, Tremont, PA
Rees Williams	b. Feb. 24, 1871, Tremont, PA	d. Feb. 24, 1872, Tremont
Joseph	b. Mar. 5, 1875, Wiconisco, PA	d. June 25, 1966, MI.

Growing up in the same house as Grandpa Joe, he would talk about his brother John and sister Lydia. Joe often told people that he was the oldest and youngest in his family of 10. This was after 1945 and all his siblings were deceased making him the oldest, and he was born last making him the youngest.

Ann was last shown in the 1880 census with the entire family living south of Pittsburgh at age 25. We have no other records for Ann. Someone wrote she died in 1935 in the family Bible. That is not a likely death date.

Jemima would marry Jacob McCormick, in 1880, and stay in the Pittsburgh area when the Harrises moved on to Illinois. She had three boys, two died young and one son Frank lived. Frank had two girls and there are descendants still living from this line. Jacob McCormick was from a well-to-do family. After marriage they lived in Sewickley, a prosperous area of Pittsburg. One newspaper article said she was out of town visiting her sister in Geneva, Wisconsin. Jacob worked for the railroad administration, and he died in 1922 while living in Kansas City. Jemima was still living near Pittsburgh. He was buried with his parents and siblings in a different cemetery than Jemima. In her younger years she used the name Rebecca. She lived in a home for Christian women in her last five years. She died in 1943 and was 86 years old. She outlived Jacob by 21 years.

John was a coal miner from a very young age starting in Tremont, to Wiconisco, to Mansfield, PA and in Braceville, Illinois. After the death of his parents Joseph & Lenah he would move with his younger sister's family to Spring Valley, Illinois where he again mined coal. When his sister's family moved back to Braceville John Moved west. He Married Carrie Gillespie in Montana. They are buried in Westoe, Montana and they were living in Red Lodge where he had been a minor. John lived to 86 years old and had no children.

Isaac T. was a coal miner at age 17 in Mansfield, Pennsylvania. Mining again with his father and brother John in Braceville, Illinois. In Braceville he married Lillian Holmes in 1990. Their first was Blanche. Their second was Clifford 7 years later. Lillian passed away before Clifford reached his first birthday. Working and raising two children was assisted by Lillian's parents. Clifford died when he was 11 years old while living with relatives as Issac was working in Chicago. Blanche was living with Mary Price (Issac's aunt), a schoolteacher. She finished high school the next year and started teaching. She moved to Decatur, IL with the Prices, where she would marry but had no children. Issac moved to Chicago and worked as a conduction on the street cars and lived with his younger sister Lydia Bates. Issac died in 1934 at age 71.

Lydia would marry Marvin Bates in Braceville in 1884 before her parents passed. They lived in Braceville, then Spring Valley, Il., back to Braceville then to Chicago. They had 4 children born in Braceville, Spring Valley, Braceville and Chicago. After the death of Joseph and Lenah the youngest, Joseph age 10, was taken in by Lydia and Marvin. Lydia also took in Isaac while living in Chicago. Lydia and Marvin also had a cottage on Lake Geneva in Wisconsin. Joe (the youngest would stay with them at the Lake as well as in Chicago until he married. There are still descendants of Lydia living.

The youngest, **Joseph**, my grandfather, would attend school and meet aunts, uncles and cousins he had never met until he arrived in Braceville. He was later taken in by his sister Lydia Bates, as he was closer in age to her children, in Chicago.

Chapter 12

Isaac & Ann Harris

Isaac Harris, my 2nd great grandfather, was married to Ann, Ann Williams or Ann Wells depending on which records you choose to follow. They were both born in the parish of Bedwellty, Monmouthshire, Wales. The original ancient parish was very large, and a number of coal mining communities grew up in this parish. They were married on Sept 8, 1823.

Isaac and Ann were the grandparents of Joseph Harris (1875-1966). From Isaac and Ann, we find twelve children all born in Tredegar, Bedwellty, Monmouthshire, Wales. Most of the male children worked in coal mining.

People moving to America usually had relatives, aunt, uncles, cousins or siblings. We have no records of Isaac or Ann concerning possible relatives arriving in America before them. Solomon, their first son, was the first of their family to arrive. He may have had uncles, aunts or cousins come before him. The stretch of mountains from Scranton to Tremont, Pennsylvania was a prime area for coal mining at that time. The Anthracite coal area covers six counties in Northeastern Pennsylvania. This covers an area of about 100 miles by 40 miles wide in the Appalachian Mountains.

The children of Isaac and Ann were:
1. Solomon Harris b. 30 Nov 1823. m. 1845 in Wales to Martha Watkins
2. Joseph Harris b. 4 Nov 1826. m. 1854 in Wales to Lenah Williams
3. Eliza Harris b 7 Jun 1829. d. after 1851
4. Enoch Harris b. 16 Mar 1831 m. 1854-55 in Scranton, PA to Sarah Jane Williams
5. Leah Harris b. 30 May 1833 m. Feb 1853 in Ebbw valley, Wales to James Davis
6. Mary Harris b. 13 Sept 1835 m. abt. 1857 in Wales to John Price.
7. Thomas Harris b. 1838. M. Kitty Bottomlee.
8. Ann Harris b. 1840. unknown
9. Isaac Harris b abt. 1842. Unknown
10. Isaac Harris II b. abt. 1844. Unknown
11. Jemmima Harris b. 1846. m. John Davis, they lived in Scranton, PA

The following account comes from the "History of Grundy County Illinois 1882" p. 112 in a biography of Solomon Harris.

Solomon Harris is a son of Isaac and Ann Harris, who came to this country in 1863; the father died in 1876. The parents had thirteen children, ten of whom grew up - Solomon, Joseph, Eliza, Enoch, Mary, Thomas, Jemima, Isaac (deceased), Leah and Isaac. When quite young, he began mining, which he followed in the old country until May 16, 1851, when he landed in October at Philadelphia, where he dug coal till January 24, 1862, when he came to Illinois and resumed his labors in a coal mine.

This account is from The Jenkins/Morgan/Harris Family Homepage:
Enoch was b. 19 March 1831, he was a miner, grocery store owner, and plasterer during his lifetime, he died in 1899 in Northeastern Pa. He met his wife Sarah Jane Williams there and they wed in abt. 1854. He came to the USA from Wales in 1851 aboard the ship" Richard Alsop". They had seven children, they were:
Ann Harris Roberts, Mary J. Harris, Morello, Thomas, Samuel, David, Jemima Harris Jenkins, and Isaac. Sarah (Enoch's wife) was a midwife and a well-known person in her community until her death in 1921 at the age of 91.

Migration to America:
Solomon (arrived 1851), (1) the eldest arrived Oct 1851 in Philadelphia, age 28. He left Wales with his wife Martha and three children and lost one child, and a 4th child was born at sea. They then had five more children born in Tremont, PA, and 4 born in Grundy, County Illinois. Solomon would move to Morris, Grundy County Illinois eleven years after arriving in Tremont. Solomon had a total of 14 children. He appears to be the first Harris to move to Illinois from Pennsylvania.

Enoch (arrived 1851), (4) the fourth child, was the only child who came to America without a wife, as he was just 20 years old. He settled near Scranton, PA where he lived his entire life. Enoch had seven children. His wife, Sarah Jane Williams could have been sister or cousin of Lenah (Williams) Harris, daughter or Reese Williams. We have identified five distant cousins by DNA through Enoch.

Joseph (arrived 1854), (2) arrived in 1854 and came directly to Tremont with his wife Lenah Williams. He was 28 and she was 21 and they had no children on arrival. They would have ten children, nine born in Tremont and the last 20 miles west in Wiconisco, PA. Four of the children died in Tremont as well as Lenah's father Rees Williams. They lived in Tremont for about 20 years, Wiconisco, PA for about two years, in what is now Carnegie, PA for about two years. Their final stop was in Braceville, IL where his siblings, Solomon, Thomas and Mary were living.

Leah (1854-57), (5) migrated to Tremont PA, with her husband James Davis and several children. Solomon & Mary had already left Tremont migrating west and she, in 1870 lived with Joseph. She then moved to Ashland, PA, about 20 miles north of Tremont, where her remaining children were born. She would have nine children all raised in Ashland, where she is buried with James. We have identified twelve distant cousins by DNA through Leah.

Mary (bef. 1857), (6) arrived in Tremont, PA shortly after her marriage to John Price. She would be 22 and John 27. They had five children, the first born in Tremont, she was the first to leave Tremont of the Harris siblings. She had three children born in Ohio in a coal mining area. Her last child Sarah was born in Illinois where she moved to be near her oldest brother Solomon. Sarah knew my grandfather Joseph (1875) when he went to school in Braceville. When Issac and Ann came to America, they lived with Mary Price in Braceville. We have identified three distant cousins by DNA through Mary.

Thomas (1857-63), (7) Probably came to America shortly after Mary and probably married in PA. His wife was Kitty Bottomlee, their first son was born in PA and the second son was born in Grundy County Illinois where they moved about the same time as Mary and Solomon. We have identified one distant cousin by DNA through Thomas.

Jemmima (1863-65), (11) was the last child to arrive at about 18 years old. I have not confirmed the following: Her husband John Davis was nine years older and could be a younger brother of James Davis. Not sure where they married but they had five children in Scranton, Pennsylvania. Again, this info is not documented.

Eliza (unknown), (3) She was 22 in the census in the 1851 in Wales

Ann (unknown), (8) She would be 23 when Isaac & Ann came to America.

Isaac (unknown), (10) He would be 19 when Isaac & Ann came to America.

In the "History of Grundy County" 1882 (p. 112) Soloman Harris states Isaac & Ann came to this country in 1863, and Issac died in 1876.

Since Ann was not listed it has been assumed that she was still alive when the book was compiled (1882). On-line family trees show her death in 1882? Ann was not listed in the 1870 census, but Isaac was living with Mary Price in Braceville. By this it would appear that Ann died before 1870. Or was living elsewhere. I do not know of any records of death. They are most likely buried in the Cotton cemetery in Braceville, Il, again no record.

Chapter 13

Ada Hazel Clark

Ada Hazel Clark was born in the Middletown, N.Y. area (possibly around Slate Hill). She was one of two twin daughters born to Cornelia (Snyder) and James M. Clark. Her twin died at birth or shortly after. She was born April 16, 1873. They were living in Middletown because that is where her father grew up and her aunt and grandparents were living there. Ada and her parents moved to Brooklyn NY before she was two years old. This is where some of her mother's siblings and her great grandmother were living. Oscar, Ward, W. Irving, Wilhelmina, Jennifer and Lotti. Her grandmother Eliza Snyder had just gotten a divorce from her husband and there was some fighting in the family and Ada'a father was in the middle of the commotion.

Ada' s only sibling, Elizabeth, was born shortly after Ada's third birthday. While they were living in Brooklyn. Elizabeth was named after their grandmother, Eliza Snyder. Ada and Hazel are not names of known ancestors.

When Ada was about 8 years old her family moved to Chicago, Illinois. Her uncle Oscar was a dentist in Chicago. Her dad had some experience in sporting goods through her uncles Ward and W. Irving while in New York found employment in Chicago in that field. In Chicago they had no electricity or indoor toilets. Ada's grandmother from NYC would live with them in Chicago at times.

From Chicago it was an easy train ride to Hartland, Michigan where Ada would go with her sister, Mother and grandmother to visit her mother's many cousins. At one occasion they stayed for two weeks getting to know their extended family. Ada's grandmother's sister was Julia Kirk, and she died long before Ada was around. The Kirk family had reunions every summer as a way to keep connected after Julia's death and the Civil war had ended. On Ada's visit to Hartland when 14 years old she obtained autographs with notes to her from her relatives. She kept the autograph book as a memento until her passing.

She graduated from Saint Vincent's school in 1890 at the age of 17. In 1890 only 3 1/2 percent of children graduated from high school. Where today a school has 160 days of school in a year, in 1890 a school year was only 86 days. There is no record of her sister graduating. Ten years out of high school Ada is working at Marshall Fields in hat sales as a milliner. Her sister is teaching piano, and both are unmarried and living at home with mom. Her father is shown in that 1900 census but from other evidence he had already moved to Kansas City by himself. Ada's grandmother Eliza was also living with the Clark family and died in 1900 before the census was taken.

Sometime after 1900, Ada met Joseph Harris who worked for the railroad as a claim's agent. He lived one block down from Ada on the same street. She at 284 Bissell St. and he at 322 Bissell St. It is interesting that in the 1900 census Ada was 26 years old and in 1910 she was 29 years old. She would maintain this age, as being born in 1881, through her marriage, every census after and her death. She had shaved eight years off her age and her sister seven years. The only ones to ever know where her sister and mother.

While dating Joseph Harris, they sometimes went on trips by railroad to a cottage on Lake Geneva, Wisconsin, which is 60 miles north of Chicago. Joseph's sister Lydia and her husband Marvin Bates owned the cottage, and Joseph lived with the Bates family.

In 1909, at 36 years old Ada, (now 28 years old) married 34-year-old Joseph. The newlyweds lived on Garfield Street in Chicago. Living with Ada was her mother and still unmarried sister. Census records do not show that Cornellia was working in 1900 or in 1910. After their first year of marriage, Ada and Joseph welcomed their first son, George Clark Harris. Two years later Robert Holbrook Harris was born in Downers Grove just outside Chicago. Two years after Ada and Joseph were married Ada's sister married Willis Mitchell in Downers Grove.

Around 1914, Joseph's job with the railroad caused the family to relocate to Battle Creek, Michigan. Ada's brother-in-law Willis Mitchell, who also worked with the railroad, had previously made the same move. Ada's mother Cornelia moved with the family to Battle Creek. So, a pattern had developed: Eliza was under the care of her daughter, Cornelia, then Cornelia was under the care of her daughter Ada. Sometime later, Ada's aunts Florence Gray and Wilhelmina Snyder joined the family residence. In 1918, Wilhelmina died leaving $2000 to Cornelia, $2300 to Florence, $400 each to Ada and Elizabeth and $100 to each of their children. At that time the two families of Harris and Mitchell bought their first car together, a 1917 Chandler nine-passenger. Willis Mitchell would be the designated driver, and the two families would go touring on weekends, usually to southwest Michigan, as Ada had a school friend who lived in Berrien Springs. MI. Most of those growing up years for Ada's two boys they lived on Main Street. Bob would tell of the garden they kept and the canning Ada did. He told of summer days when his dad would take the inter-urban train to Beadle Lake to fish for bluegill. He would bring home a mess of fish and Ada would clean and cook them. This had to bring back memories of her father James who when living in Chicago would go bass fishing every weekend. Bringing fish home every weekend sure helped Ada know how to clean and prepare them.

In those summer days in Battle Creek, the two young boys were active in the Boy Scouts, which had recently been started by Baden Powell who lived in nearby Marshall, MI. Ada and Joseph's family would often rent a cottage for one week on the east end of Saint Mary's Lake. Joseph and Ada, their boys, grandma Cornelia, and Aunt Florence made great memories at that cabin going fishing, swimming, and splashing in the lake.

In 1940, 90-year-old Ada's mother Cornelia died. At that time, Cornelia was living at Ada's younger sister Elizabeth's home in Battle Creek. She had moved from Ada's for the winter, as it was warmer at Elizabeth's house. The following year, Ada died from cancer. She is buried at Memorial Park Cemetery in Battle Creek, MI. Ada's husband Joseph went to live with their son George, his wife Elizabeth, and their family until his death in 1966.

Chapter 14

Cornelia Johnson Snyder

Cornelia Johnson Snyder, my great grandmother, was born January 12, 1850, in the Round Hill district of Greenwich, Connecticut. Round Hill is a 90-minute walk, uphill, from Greenwich, about 5.5 miles. She was the fifth of nine children born to William D. Snyder and Eliza Brown. The house she was born and raised in was her grandmother's, Elizabeth (Betsy) Brown. It was a 36-acre farm where they had a horse, two milch cows, two pigs, and many chickens. They grew wheat, Indian corn, hay, oats and Irish Potatoes. Irish potatoes were a new crop in Connecticut as prior to the Irish potato, potatoes were used as pig feed. The pink fir apple potato is the only potato still available today from the 1850s. They had an orchard and raised garden crops and produced 125 pounds of butter. Her father spent much of his time on the road as he was a dentist and went to populated areas to find clients. The year she was born her father was shown in two census records, one at Round Hill and another in New Cannon, Connecticut, about 13 miles east of Round Hill. The year before her birth the railroad was completed for New York City to New Haven Connecticut.

Their home was handed down through several generations and was very small by today's standards. A front room was the living area where you ate and baked on the brick fireplace. This was also where visitors would meet. Behind the fireplace was the main bedroom (possibly two bedrooms). With eight people in the house and more on the way, it was very crowded. The house was on the northwest corner of Buckfield Lane and John Street. She would

start public school at the Round Hill, one room school, less than 1/4 of a mile east. It was next to the cemetery where her grandfather, Nehemiah Brown was buried. Her school day was from 9 am to 2 pm and covered only 120 days a year, and only through the 8th grade. This allowed for more time to work around the farm.

When Cornelia was 12 years old her, oldest cousin Newton Kirk (24) came to visit. He was living in NYC and grew up in Heartland, Michigan. The Civil War had just begun, and Newton and her brother Oscar (19) decided to join the Grand Army of the Republic. Oscar in Connecticut and Newton went back to Michigan to fight with his friends. Three years later Cornelia's father would travel to Annapolis, Maryland to bring home her brother Oscar. After months in the army hospital, he could come home. He was described as nothing but skin and bones. Both Oscar and Newton had survived imprisonment at Andersonville prison in Georgia.

At least three of Cornelia's sisters were schoolteachers. It does not appear that Cornelia did any teaching. This area of Connecticut was heavy into hat making in Danbury and shoe making in New Canaan. In New Canaan shoe making was a cottage industry where shoemakers including women would work from their home and take their finished work to the factory and pick up more raw materials. In census records we see many shoemakers who lived in the Round Hill area. It is possible Cornelia had some experience in this area. When she was 16 years old, her oldest brother Irving was co-owner of "Peck and Snyder" Sporting Goods in NYC. Family tale is that she tied baseballs at P & S. Tying baseballs would be similar to tying shoes. This is the most likely place for her to have met a salesman, James Clark. Cornelia's oldest brother Oscar carried on the tradition of their father as a dentist after the war. It was said that Oscar ground off all of Cornelia's teeth, top and bottom so they would all fit flat together. This would have been done before she was 30 years old.

Cornelia came from a close-knit family with many cousins on her mother's side. Many times, all the nine children would side with their mother Eliza when conflicts arose between her parents. Cornelia and her siblings had an aunt (her mother's sister) who died when Cornelia was only five. The aunt Julia Brown Kirk lived in Hartland, Livingston County, Michigan. Over the years Eliza, Cornelia and other siblings made their way to the Kirk's family reunions. This from The Livingston Herald, Aug 16, 1887: *"Parshallville, A Mrs. Clark and two daughters from Chicago, have been visiting at the Kirk's in this vicinity."* The reunions started in 1869 and lasted well over 100 years. Most years there would be 60 to 100 family members present.

Cornelia married James M. Clark in December of 1871 in Greenwich. Cornelia's siblings were living in Greenwich and NYC at that time and James' family lived in Middletown, New York. James and Cornelia would move to Middletown, NY where she had her first child Ada. Cornelia had twin girls, but the second girl died at or shortly after birth. They would then move to NYC where two years later her daughter Elizabeth was born. While in NYC, James worked in the family sporting goods business. At the time of Elizabeth's birth, Cornelia's parents, William and Eliza, got a divorce. Then Eliza moved with her two youngest daughters to NYC to be near the rest of the children and their families. W. Irving, Ward, Oscar, Willamina, and Cornellia were all living in NYC. Ida and Florence, both schoolteachers, were in Cos Cob near Greenwich, CT. These were hectic years from 1875 to 1882 in the Snyder family. The family left Round Hill leaving everything behind then went back to get things out of the house while their dad (William) was still there. There were conflicts between Oscar and their dad as well as James and their dad. Soon followed the death of her first sibling (Oscar).

Cornelia would have no more children, and her husband James always wanted a son, but it never happened. James and Cornelia moved to Chicago around 1880. She would be 30 years old, and the girls would be 4 and 7 years old. They would live together with the girls, in Chicago, for the next 20 years.

While living in Chicago, Eliza, Cornelia's mother, passed away (March 23, 1900). Her body was sent back to Greenwich for burial. We do not know how long Eliza had been living with James and Cornelia, but Cornelia was the only sibling living in Chicago at the time of her death. All of Cornelia's siblings still live in the east. I imagine that Eliza would move from family to family in her later years. It was at this time (1900) that James decided to take a new job in Kansas City. James worked in sporting goods and in the promotion of fishing he would spend every weekend and some weeks of the summer fishing in Illinois, Wisconsin and Michigan. He worked during the week and was gone on weekends. The girls now 24 and 27 were unmarried and still living at home. Cornelia would not leave the girls, and a sharp division came between Cornelia and James. There are no photos of James remaining and Cornelia would now consider herself as a widow.

Cornelia's eldest daughter Ada would marry Joseph Harris, also of Chicago, on April 29, 1909. One year later Cornelia's youngest daughter Elizabeth would marry Willis Halem Mitchell. Joseph and Ada would reside with Cornelia after their marriage. By 1913 Ada, Joseph, their two boys and Cornelia would move to Battle Creek Michigan where Elizabeth and Willis were living. Willis worked for the Grand Trunk railroad and Joseph for American Express. A couple of years later they would rent a bigger house, on Main Street, and Cornelia's sisters Wilhelmina and Florence would move from the New York City area to Battle Creek to spend their retirement years together, with Cornelia.

Cornelia's oldest sister Wilhelmina died in 1917 and left the bulk of her money to her two nieces, Ada and Elizabeth. From that money the two families of Joseph Harris, Willis Mitchell with Florence and Cornelia bought their first automobile owned jointly but driven by Willis, a 1917 Chandler, a nine-passenger touring car. Cornelia, Florence, Joseph and Ada Harris and their two boys George and Robert spent one week each summer at a cottage on Fine Lake, north of Battle Creek. This year was remembered as the year that a telegram came for Cornelia telling her that James Clark had passed away presumably in Kansas City.

Cornelia's sister Florence Gray, passed away in 1935. Cornelia was the last of the nine Snyder siblings to pass. Cornelia died February 7, 1940, of pneumonia at Elizabeth's house where she had moved for the winter as Elizabeth kept the house warmer than Ada. She is buried in a plot owned by Joseph Harris in the Masonic section of the Memorial Park Cemetery in Battle Creek. Next to her is her sister, Florence. Cornelia lived in Greenwich, CT, New York City, Philadelphia, Chicago and Battle Creek

I found the following story on-line. It is a good representation of how a 10-year-old girl would have experienced school in 1860.

'The crow of the rooster awakens our family. The light of this very cool day begins to reveal itself. It's dawn on Monday, in early November 1860. It's time to rise, feed the farm animals, harvest some vegetables, and get ready for school.

The morning activities are complete, so our mother hands us our lunch pails, and we begin our walk to school. My younger siblings who are in first and fourth grades join me on the walk, only a 1/10 of a mile each way. As we get closer, we can hear the ringing of the school bell, indicating that school will begin in a few minutes.

We arrive at the one-room schoolhouse and enter. My younger brother has to sit on the opposite side of the schoolhouse, as boys and girls are separated during the school day. We are arranged by grade, with the younger grades sitting in the front rows, closer to the teacher and the 30-star flag. Our school has about 16 kids, ranging from grades one to eight.

Before we get started with learning, we have to finish our schoolhouse chores and set up for the day. I normally go to the well to fill the crock with drinking water. My younger male sibling gets wood for the wood-burning stove, while my younger female sibling sweeps the floor.

Today, we are finishing some reading, and doing some writing, history, geography, and arithmetic on our slate boards. The best part of the day is spelling, as we sometimes do a fun spelling bee contest among the older kids.

I am interrupted during my reading to take my younger sister outside to the girl's outhouse. It starts to rain. The short walk home will be longer and dismal. Want to join us?'

Chapter 15

William D. Snyder

William D. Snyder was born around 1818 in New York state. Two records show William as being born in Dutchess Co, NY. Until recently Williams' parents were unknown. His third marriage record in 1882 in NYC shows his father as William and Mother as Phebe Owen. Charles B. Snyder d. 1915 could be related but we have not made a connection yet as he is buried in the same plot as William. We have only one small photo. He appears to be a thin, short person. He was very articulate, several times defended himself in court, and wrote articles in local newspapers.

This biography will be divided into sections of Marriages, Court actions and conflicts, Employment, Interesting findings, where he lived and died.

Marriages (3):

William Snyder married Eliza Jane Brown. On Feb. 11, 1837, in NYC (UMC records), they had nine children together. After 36 years of marriage Eliza moved out of the home on the property given to her by her father. She took her four youngest children with her to NYC. It took two years to finalize the divorce in December 1975. The real separation actually began ten year earlier. Terms like cruelty, neglect, hitting, kicking, beating and bruised, profane and harsh language were part of this divorce. From the time of the divorce their nine children all sided with their mother.

William must have had a sweet side as well as a confrontational, nasty side. Connecticut divorce law permits remarriage. Less than one year after his divorce from Eliza he married Adeline R Haight (UMC) in NYC. She may have lived in Greenwich and left her husband for Dr. Snyder (speculation). William was 58 and Adeline was 18 years younger.

His second marriage was short lived, as six years later on Aug 24,1882 William remarried, Carrie (Caroline) L. Deisenbury. This marriage was even shorter. William was 63 and Carrie was 25 years younger. Carrie had her mother and brother move in with William. After three years of marriage William gave Carrie an ultimatum. Either Carrie or her mother had to move out. Carrie and her mother left together, and William agreed to pay her $5 each week. After a year of payments William stopped paying support. William claimed because he was aging, and business was slow he could not pay her. The court reduced Williams support payment to $1.50 per week.

Court actions and conflicts:

It seems William was in and out of court most of his life, in addition around his divorces. His father-in-law Nehemiah Brown clearly wrote William out of the Round Hill property after he had married Eliza. Elizabeth Brown, step-mother of Eliza, allowed Williams' family to live with her. Their differences required court action requiring Elizabeth to pay William for the furniture in the house. When the one-room school burned down at Round Hill there was heated debate over whether to rebuild with another one-room school or build a two-room school. William was at the center of that debate. William was taken to court over a matter where a carriage driver (taxi) said something inappropriate to his daughter taking her to Round Hill. Apparently, he did not hit the driver but his actions and language were outside the law? Not sure who won. Eliza locked him out of the house at Round Hill the summer before their divorce. He spent the summer in a hotel in town. He didn't pay his bill and went to court as the hotel tried to collect. Apparently, after his divorce with Eliza, he had a judgement for the house furniture Eliza left at Round Hill. William got a judgement against his son-in-law James keeping him away from William. He then got a judgment against James after James took the furniture from Round Hill. His son Oscar took him to court because he opened some of Oscar's mail and once again the whole Snyder family despised William.

Employment: (dentist, farmer & publisher)

William was a dentist all of his life. I assume he served an apprenticeship when he started. He worked in NYC when he first married. He would have started dentistry around 1835-37. The world's first dental school, in Baltimore, was not even started until 1840. I would imagine most dental work involved pulling teeth to eliminate pain. In 1844, a Connecticut dentist was the first to discover that nitrous oxide can be used as anesthesia. Moving to Round hill after his first three children were born, put him away from an office to work out of. He would have offices in New Canaan, CT, Troy, NY, White Plains, NY, Peekskill, NY and ending up back in NYC at the corner of Fulton and Franklin in Brooklyn. In 1833-1850, two brothers from France introduced amalgam filling material in the United States under the name *Royal Mineral Succedaneum*. The brothers are charlatans whose unscrupulous methods spark the "amalgam wars," a bitter controversy within the dental profession over the use of amalgam fillings. In 1844, it was reported that fifty percent of all dental restorations placed in upstate New York consisted of amalgam. However, at that point the use of dental amalgam was declared to be malpractice. (50% Mercury) By 1860 William had his son Oscar working with him. In 1871, the first commercially manufactured foot-treadle dental engine was patented. In the 1880s, the collapsible metal tube revolutionized toothpaste manufacturing and marketing. Dentifrice had been available only in liquid or powder form, usually made by individual dentists, and sold in bottles, porcelain pots, or paper boxes. Tube toothpaste, in contrast, is mass-produced in factories, mass-marketed, and sold nation-wide. In twenty years, it had become the norm. In William Snyder's era, he would have sold or made dentifrices to sell to the public. Advertisements indicated Wm D. Snyder also performed crowns on teeth. "The greatest achievement of dental science (gas 50 cents extra)".

When William was 32, he was found in the census at Round Hill and also in the census at New Canaan, CT. While he was in New Canaan, he published a newspaper. Newspapers in nearby towns were so solidly Whig and opposing tickets were seldom mentioned. So, for the first time in history New Canaan published a newspaper, *The New Canaan Omnibus & Fairfield County Agriculturist*, dated Apr. 2, 1851. The editor was William D. Snyder, the local part-time dentist. Although the stated purpose of the *Omnibus* was to open its columns to all political parties if they paid for the space occupied by their views, the only party represented was the Free Soil, which listed its statewide slate. Both local Free-Soil candidates went down to defeat when New Canaan went Democratic that first week in April 1851, and since the first was also the last issue of the *Omnibus*, little more is known of local anti-slave activities.

When William was 38, he took some time off from dentistry and went on what we would call a timeshare sales promotion. In early 1856 William traveled to Nicaragua to investigate free land for farmers. Newspapers around the world published a letter he wrote describing his near-death experience traveling to Nicaragua. He would travel from NYC with a boat load of mostly men to Granada, Nicaragua. They were trying to lure Americans by a golden promise held out by Nicaragua. They were also looking for carpenters and men for their military. Since William had his 36-acre farm at Round Hill he went to check out the free 300 acres of land being offered. William became acquainted with eight other Connecticut farmers on the boat ride there. Upon arrival all accommodations were full. He went to the American conciliate with no luck. However, he and a companion went and bought hammocks and hung them in the trees behind the conciliate. He found an American who bought a house, and he took in William and others. One Connecticut farmer sold his land before he came to Nicaragua – an unfortunate choice as he would die from the fever in three days. Four of the Connecticut farmers went out on a three-day trip to survey the land, by donkey. Only two returned as two died of fever. Another died three days later. Another day, William visited a shop where carpenters were fabricating caskets. The carpenter he talked to died that night and was buried in his own casket. One day he went to visit the military base to find many Americans living in poverty with no means to return home. Their pay was barely enough to pay their laundry bill. The 300 acres William was shown needed to be cleared and one person would take a year to clear five acres. Of the eight people he met, only three were able to return alive to New York. In the city of Granada there were 400 Americans, and they were dying at a rate of five per day.

Interesting findings:

Charles B. Snyder (d.1916) is buried in a plot owned by Williams' son Irving in the Putnam cemetery in Greenwich. We cannot make a connection with Charles and don't know if or how he would be related but Charles was a newspaper owner. He may have helped William produce the 1851 newspaper.

Snyder's homestead was at Round Hill, Greenwich, Connecticut. Round Hill is basically the top of the hill as the ground rises from Greenwich north about five miles. The 1867 Bear's map of North Greenwich shows Dr. Snyder as being at the end of a dead-end road just north (less than ½ mile) of the Methodist church at the top of Round Hill. This land was inherited by Eliza from her father Nehemiah Brown (will dated 1839). That will clearly stated that it was to go to Eliza then to her children (not William).

A story written by Eliza's nephew Newton Kirk tells of visiting the Snyder family at Round Hill before he or Oscar signed up for the Civil War service. In 1865, William went to Annapolis, MD to pick up his son, Oscar who survived a year-long imprisonment in a confederate prison. By 1866, Oscar was working with his dad again in the dental trade. William was detested by all the children, who sided with Eliza. I find it strange to see that on Feb. 25th, 1891 he attended the wedding of Ward's daughter in Long Branch, NJ.

The 1870 agriculture census shows William Snyder had the following on the 36 acres at Round Hill: one horse, two cows, two pigs. They grew wheat, hay, oats, potatoes, orchard fruit and garden produce. They produced 150 pounds of butter. The 1850 census was very similar.

Where He Lived:

Until he was married at age 19, we have no idea where he grew up. He lived in NYC for seven years at the time of his marriage. Then he moved to Round

Hill, Greenwich, Connecticut until around 1876- a span of over 30 years. About three years in that span, he moved to White Plains, NY (7 miles west) because of conflict with his mother-in-law.

In May 1874, Eliza moved out of Round Hill with their remaining four children. William stayed there for two more years until the divorce was final in December 1875 and the property was sold. William had purchased other parcels of land around Round Hill over the years. William would live in Brooklyn, NYC from 1876 (age 62) until after 1891 which is the last location we found him. The last newspaper record was Sept. 9, 1891, Brooklyn Daily Eagle, an incident involving a missing bicycle where he was a witness.

William died on March 17, 1894, in Stamford, CT. He is buried in Greenwich, Putnam Cemetery. At the time of his death William had two daughters living in Greenwich but no children were living in Stamford. He could have been in an asylum but that is only speculation. The plot in Putnam cemetery was purchased by W. Irving Snyder at the time of Williams death. Six years later Eliza (divorced wife) died in Chicago and was buried next to William. In 1916 an unknown Charles B. Snyder was added to the plot. In 1978 a granddaughter Dorothy Eldridge Cotter was buried in the same cemetery plot. Her's is the only grave headstone on the plot.

Recently, I also found a William D. Snyder death record from Stamford, Ct. He died on March 17, 1894, a resident of Glenbrook at the age of 76. No parents were given, and he was a dentist. Cause of death was Chronic Cystitis or (UTI). Urinary tract infections (UTI) have been found to be associated with a variety of neuropsychiatric disorders. Dr Givens of Stamford had a facility in Stamford where he treated neuropsychiatric disorders. So perhaps Wm. Snyder did not have syphilis as our cousin Lucille thought. It was probably more likely wishful thinking as the entire family sided with Eliza his first wife.

William D. Snyder timeline:
1819 William D. Snyder born Dutchess Co. New York.
1937 Age 20 Practiced dentistry NYC. Usually learned through apprenticeship.
1837 Age 20 Married Eliza Brown NYC.
1838 Age 21 Birth of first child Wilhelmina. The first 3 of his 9 children were born in NYC.
1847 Age 30 Moves family to Round Hill where he lives with his mother-in-law (Betsy) in the house where Nehemiah lived and raised his 3 daughters.
1848 Age 31 First of 4 children born at Round Hill. Ida, Cornelia, Ward & Florence.
1850 Age 33 Wm. has a second residence in New Canaan, Ct where he has a

dentist office. He published the first newspaper supporting "Free Soil" party.

1855   Age 35 Death of Eliza's sister Julia, who was to receive 1/3 of Brown estate.
1856   Age 39 Traveled to Nicaragua, in March to investigate free land for farmers.
1859   Age 42 Moved seven miles west to White Plains, NY.
1860   Age 43 Practicing dentistry with son Oscar in Port Chester, NY. 8 miles south.
1864   Age 47 Moves to New house at Round Hill ½ mile north of Nehemiah's old home. This is likely the watercolor that Wilhelmina painted in 1887
1865   Age 48 Wm. Goes to Annapolis, MD Hospital to bring his son Oscar home.
1871   Age 54 Embroiled in a campaign for a new two-room school at Round Hill.
1873   Age 56 January Wm. in trouble with law over his confrontation with a taxi driver who had harassed his daughter riding from the train station to Round Hill.
1874   Age 57 Death of Eliza's sister Sarah, who received 1/3 of Brown estate.
1874   Age 57 May, Eliza moves out of Round Hill home with youngest children.
1875   Age 58 Divorce finalizes after 10 years of problems. Fairfield Co. records.
1875   Age 58 James Clark (son-in-law) gathers furniture from Round Hill home and takes it to Brooklyn where most of the family now lives.
1876   Age 59 January newspaper reports Wm. has sold all his and his wife's property at Round Hill.
1876   Age 59 Wm. remarries Adeline Haight who is 19 years younger in NYC.
1881   Age 64 Embroiled in conflict with Oscar in NYC children sided with Eliza.
1882   Age 65 Wm. remarries Carrie Dusenbury who is 26 years younger in NYC.
1891   Age 74 Wm. Snyder attended the wedding of Ward's Daughter, in Branchport, NJ. He was still living in Brooklyn at that time.
1894   Age 77 Wm. died in Stamford, CT., March 17.

William Snyder Visits Nicaragua

"A Visit to Nicaragua", was the title in a newspaper article found in various newspapers from New York to Australia, between March and August 1856. The article is a letter written by William D. Snyder, a Connecticut farmer. This is my summary of the letter written by William D. Snyder.

It appears that Dr. Snyder went on an investigative trip to Nicaragua to see what all the fuss was about. Much like a timeshare sales pitch of today. I am guessing that the new Nicaragua Government was trying to lure Americans to Nicaragua to bolster the new government which had been taken over by "General Walker" an American who had overthrown the prior government the year before. So, farmers, carpenters, and military personnel took the free trip to Nicaragua.

It appears Dr. Snyder was there for about two weeks, that being fourteen more days than he wanted. He did not actually say that. Dr. Snyder would be 38 years old, had five children between 3 and 14 at home. He was a dentist and he or his family farmed a 40-acre plot in Greenwich, Connecticut.

Farmers: Dr. Snyder was accompanied by another farmer who had sold his place in Connecticut to venture out into this new frontier. Snyder met eight American farmers on the ship "Northern Light" arriving at Granada. Nicaragua was offering American farmers 250 to 300 acres to farm to settle. It was labeled the "Garden of the World". Snyder's newfound friend from Connecticut died in three days. Four of the eight farmers went out for three days to investigate land. Two died and two returned to Granada. Three days later the third died. Snyder describes the land as being covered with underbrush, snakes and scorpions. It would take a year to make five acres fertile. The government kept the most fertile land.

The most lucrative employment for a carpenter was building coffins for the government. One carpenter got sick at 6 o'clock in the evening and died by 4 am. He was buried that day in the same coffin he had made. He was in excellent health.

Men recruited for the military died at an alarming rate. From Granada they would march to Leon. Snyder describes soldiers in tears, over their desolate situation. Soldiers earn barely enough money to pay for their laundry.

Snyder describes a man who came down with the fever, on the ship, on the way home, died and his body thrown overboard.

In the end Snyder guesses there are about 400 Americans in Granada, and they were dying at the rate of about five a day.

I would say he was a lucky guy to make it back to Connecticut where he would have three more children.

Chapter 16

Eliza (Elizabeth) Jane Brown

Eliza Brown was born Mar 28, 1815, at Round Hill, Greenwich, CT. She was the daughter of Nehemiah Brown Jr who is buried in the Round Hill Methodist Church cemetery. Nehemiah b.1860, d. 1840. Eliza had two sisters- three and five years older, Julia (Brown) Kirk, and Sarah P. (Brown) Ford. A good source of evidence comes from Nehemiah Brown's will for 1839 where he divides his estate, at Round Hill, into three parcels for the three girls after his death in 1940. Her middle name Jane is from her family (George, Robert, and Lucille). I have no formal documentation for her middle name. Information from her sister Julia's family (John Kirk) mentions that Eliza would visit them in Michigan, and they referred to her as Jane. In her fathers will there is a clear distinction between the three girls and their spouses. It would appear that her father Nehemiah did not like her husband William Snyder and clearly cut him out of any land inheritance.

Eliza's mother is still in question. All evidence from internet sources, (ancestry, Roots web, LDS etc.) points to Sarah Purdy. The Barbour Collection (old New England record) indicated Nehemiah married Sarah, Sept 3, 1797. That marriage was also recorded in the "New York Monthly". Julia was born in 1810; Sarah was born in 1812. In 1840, when Nehemiah died, Elizabeth, also called Betsy, was his wife. Elizabeth Brown was also living with the Snyders at Round Hill in the 1850 census. We have never found a death or marriage record to certify the mother of Eliza.

Eliza married William D. Snyder on February 11, 1837 at a Methodist Episcopal Church in NYC. She would have been 18 or 19 and William one year younger than her at the time of their marriage. Their first three children were born in NYC. before moving to Round Hill, Greenwich, CT.

Family tradition has always been that there is some Indian ancestry in the line of Eliza Jane. Several in our family have no wisdom teeth. A DNA (mtDNA) was done for Robert Harris as he is the only one left which would have DNA directly from his mother's mother's mother, etc. That test did not show any evidence of an Indian blood line.

Eliza was apparently the driving force in the Snyder Family. She had nine children (one died young). All were educated. The women married well, and the men were in business. Round Hill is located on the eastern border of Connecticut along the Boston Post Road which was the main road for troops from Boston to NYC in the Revolution. In the early 1800 Round Hill was a remote location. Even after trains were built prior to the Civil war it was five miles from the train uphill to Round Hill. Today, Round Hill is covered with multimillion dollar homes. At one point during the Civil War, Eliza's nephew Newton was stationed in NYC. Newton was Eliza's sister Julia's son from Hartland, MI. Eliza went down to visit Newton at the military base near NYC. Can you imagine her going there by herself by horse and train and carriage? Eliza invited Newton to come up to Round Hill for the weekend before he was to head south for the war. Newton could not get off for the weekend. Eliza went to the base commander and got Newton off for the weekend. What a woman!

Consider this, Eliza's husband was William D. Snyder, and he was a dentist. While living at Round Hill, William was gone much of the time. There was not much dental work at Round Hill, he would have to spend weeks at an office in Westchester, Poughkeepsie, New Cannon, or NYC. Eliza would raise the children, teach them, and see that the 36-acre farm was worked. One Agricultural census showed they had one horse, two milch cows, two pigs, and produced 100 bushels of corn, 25 bushels of potatoes, 40 bushels of apples, 24 bushels of garden produce, made 150 pounds of butter along with 6 tons of hay on their 36 acres. I assume they also had chickens and eggs as the census does not ask.

Eliza and William divorced in 1875 when most of the four children were still living at Round Hill. Eliza got no money in the divorce and quickly moved to NYC. The divorce process started ten years prior. In 1881, in the New York Times, William Snyder (dentist) was accused of opening his son's mail. From the New York Times May 13, 1881, states that Eliza was separated from William B. Snyder and the children all sided with Eliza.

Eliza may have lived with Cornelia in New York City in 1883. She likely shared time with her other adult children in NYC and Connecticut. She died in Chicago on March 22, 1900, while living with Cornelia's family. She was buried on March 23 in Greenwich. Cemetery records from Putnam Cemetery show Elizabeth Snyder buried in Lot 79 which was purchased by W. Irving Snyder in 1885.

Timeline of Eliza:
Age 21 Married William D. Snyder in NYC (1837)
Age 23 first Child Wilhelmina born NYC (1838)
Age 27 second child born Oscar E. NYC (1842)
Age 29 #3 child born, Washington Irving NYC (1844)
Age 30 Moves family to Round Hill where she lives with his mother (Betsy).
Age 32 Eliza's oldest sister Julia Kirk moves from RH to Michigan (1847)
Age 33 #4 child born, Ida Frances (Lockwood, Green) Round Hill (1848)
Age 35 #5 child born, Cornelia Johnson (Clark) Round Hill (1850)
Age 35 Death of Eliza's sister Julia, who was to receive 1/3 of Brown estate.
Age 37 #6 child born, Ward Beecher at Round Hill (1852)
Age 43 #7 child born, Florence (Frank) Comstock (Gray) Round Hill (1858)
Age 44 #8 child born, Jennifer at White Plains NY (1859)
Age 47 Last child born, Lottie L (Finney) at White Plains NY (1861)
Age 48 visited by nephew Newton Kirk at Round Hill
Age 50 marriage of W. Irving (oldest son)
Age 52 marriage of Oscar, Stamford CT. (1867)
Age 53 marriage of Ida to Green
Age 54 Death of Elizabeth (Betsy) Brown at Round Hill.
Age 56 marriage of Cornelia to Clark in Greenwich (1871)
Age 60 gets a divorce from William D. Snyder (1875)
Age 62 lived in NYC at same address as Ward and Cornelia
Age 61 marriage of Ward (NJ)(1876)
Age 64 lived in NYC (Brooklyn) Boarder (1880 census)
Age 67 death of Oscar, NM buried in Stamford CT (1882)
Age 69 marriage of Lottie to Finney Manhattan, NY (1884)
Age 73 2nd marriage of Ida to Lockwood (1888)
Age 76 Sold 7 acres at RH to Irving for $1
Age 76 2nd marriage of Florence to Gray Stamford CT (1894)
Age 79 death of divorced husband William (1894)
Age 85 died Chicago Il, buried Greenwich CT (1900)

Brick Wall: Who was the mother of Eliza Brown? Sarah Purdy or Elizabeth

Eliza Brown Birth date 28 Mar 1815 from Gedcom file from descendants of Ward. Eliza's siblings: Sarah P. Brown Ford, b. 1812 from death notice 9 May 1874 Manhattan.

Julia Brown Kirk, b. 10 July 1810, d. 1955 Hartland, Livingston Co., MI

Nehemiah Brown Jr. as the father of the three girls, from his will and probate record, Stanford, CT 8 Jun 1839 and a second probate record in Greenwich in 1870.

Over 150 genealogy records show the mother to be Sarah Purdy on Ancestry.com with only a marriage record from 13 years before the girls were born as evidence.

Sarah Purdy: From the Hale collection: Sarah (or Sally) Purdy married Nehemiah Brown, 3 Sep 1797 in Greenwich. Sarah's birth is given as 16 Jun 1776 in the Barbour collection.

Problem: Sarah may have died before the girls were born as the only record, we have is her marriage.

If Sarah was the mother of Julia, she would have been 34 years old and married for 13 years before having her first child? People back then did not have birth control and usually did not wait to start their family.

In the Burying Hill cemetery at Round Hill, Greenwich we find the following on "Find a Grave". There is a headstone that is rather crude, on slate, rather than white stone. It reads, S. P. B. 11 April 1799. I have contacted the photographer of the stone, and he distinctly remembers that the headstone was there as he had to remove some dirt to see the complete date.

Looking for who is buried in the Burying Hill cemetery by different accounts. The Hale collection is the most common. However, another record is from Francis F. Spies page 103 and 194 cemetery inscriptions 1931, found in Family Search. In this listing there are two interesting things. 1. This listing was not called the Burying Hill Cemetery. It was "Jonathan Knapp Yard", "on road going east just north of M. E. Church at Round Hill". 2. From that record #I344 was Nehemiah Brown, #I345 was Sophia Brown and #I346 (Sally Purdy, his wife, m. 13 Sep. 1797). This record basically says entry 1346 was the Sarah wife of Nehemiah Jr. is buried in this cemetery. This is where her husband's parents are interned. This would support that S. P. B. could be the Sarah Purdy who married Nehemiah Brown Jr.

Elizabeth: From June 8, 1839, the will of Nehemiah Brown (Stamford, CT) shows his property at Round Hill, Greenwich. Elizabeth was to receive all of Nehemiah's real and personal property for all of her natural life. After her death the property was to be divided into 1/3's for Julia, Sarah and Eliza. From census records she would have been born in abt. 1794 in Connecticut. From her death record in Greenwich her parents were Susan and Minor (no last name) and she was 79 and her name was shown as Betsie. From this she would have been born in 1790. She would then have been 20 years old at the birth of Julia (1810).

Problem: Elizabeth (Betsy) has no marriage record.

Round Hill M.E. Church started in 1810 but membership records only list those who were members between 1810 and 1858 as a group. Members include Nehemiah Brown, Sarah Brown and Betsy Brown. From an abstract of church records of the town of Greenwich 1913 p.136 (Mead) from Lib. of Congress. Also shows John & Julia Kirk as members. Sarah Brown could be Nehemiah's daughter or his first wife. One church record showed the members listed alphabetically. A second record appeared to members buy when they joined, and it showed Nehemiah and Betsie together.

In the 1800 to 1850 census the head of the house is listed by name, then the occupants by age and gender only (with no names). Nehemiah's census record of 1800:

	Census Record	Possible person fitting this description
Nehemiah	1 boy >10:	Unknown (could this be Ruth Purdy's child?)
	1 Male 26-44:	Nehemiah Brown Jr. age 40
	1 Male 45 up:	Nehemiah Brown Sr., age 74
	1 female 26-44	Ruth Purdy (Nehemiah's sister-in-law) (28) *
	1 female 45 up	Ruth (Peck) Purdy (Nehemiah's mother-in-law) age 54
	Not listed	Sarah Purdy Brown age 24 if alive?

Sarah Purdy's father passed away 17 years earlier than this census and Ruth (Caleb Sr.'s wife, Sarah's mother) raised four children (Ruth, Caleb, Sarah and Elias). Sarah's oldest brother Caleb died 5 years earlier. Two years earlier after one year of marriage to Nehemiah Jr., Sarah and Nehemiah purchased 10 acres of land at Round Hill from Ruth Purdy, Sarah's mother. So, in 1800 Sarah's mother Ruth Purdy was living with Nehemiah Jr where she had been living when her daughter Sarah was alive (speculation). Sarah's sister Ruth was 28 in 1800, living in the same house as her mother and now deceased sister and still unmarried. She would later marry Nathaniel Knapp in 1815.

The following information is drawn from the 1810 Census. Living at Round Hill (Greenwich) Connecticut was Major Brown, Nehemiah Jr Brown next to each other and 7 houses up is Ruth Purdy (sister or mother of Sarah?)

	Census Record	Possible person fitting this description
Nehemiah Brown:	1 Male 45 up:	Nehemiah Brown Jr., age 50
	1 girl >10:	Julia Brown (>1) b. Jul 10
	1 female 16-26:	Sarah Purdy would be 34, Betsy would be 20
	1 other person:	Worker?

Looking at this record of Nehemiah Brown It appears that Betsy is the mother of Julia Brown, not Sarah Purdy.

From the 1820 census we find Nehemiah with 3 girls and a wife between 26 and 45. This census cannot discern between Sarah Purdy age 44 and Betsy age 30. It is interesting that Nehemiah Knapp was living 7 houses down from Major the same distance that Ruth Purdy was living in 1810, and next to him was Elias Purdy (brother of Sarah Purdy Brown).

Family records: From the side of Eliza, we recognize Nehemiah as Eliza's father but have no handed down history of her mother. Julia who died in 1855. Her family records handed down through the years show her mother as Elizabeth.

Conclusion: By census records alone Sarah Purdy could not have been the mother of Eliza Brown. This alone disqualifies over 150 records on Ancestry which show Sarah as the mother of Julia, Sarah and Eliza. In fact, Nehemiah did marry Sarah Purdy but she most likely died before the 1800 census.

Chapter 17

Children of William D. Snyder & Eliza Brown

William and Eliza were married in NYC on Feb 11, 1837. They would have nine children over a span of 25 years- three boys and six girls. This is a brief summary of each child.

Wilhelmina Snyder was the first-born January 12th, 1838, in NYC.

When she was 10 years old, she moved with her brothers Oscar and Irving with their parents to Round Hill, Greenwich, CT. Wilhelmina became a schoolteacher and may have taught in a one- or two-room school in the Greenwich area. She would move early in her life to NYC where she was a teacher. In 1860 her cousin Newton Kirk, who was two years older than her, was also living in NYC. She and Newton and Wilhelmina's mother would visit famous Christian preachers from NYC and Philadelphia. When she was 27 years old her brother Irving who was just 21 cofounded "Peck & Snyder" sporting goods. She may have been a silent partner (investor) in her brother's indever. At the time of her death, she still owned stock in "Spaulding" sports, who had purchased "Peck & Snyder". She retired from teaching in the early 1900s. In 1908 she requested that Newton write her an account of his time in the civil war. In 1914 she moved to Battle Creek, Michigan where she lived with two sisters, Cornelia and Florence, a niece Ada, her husband Joseph Harris and their two boys George and Robert. She is most remembered for the watercolor paintings she left to her sister Cornelia's family when she died in June of 1918. There was about $6000 in her estate at her death. Money was given to George and Robert Harris, Lucille and Raymond Mitchell, Ada and Elizabeth Clark, Emma and Jessie Snyder as well as her two sisters. $6000 in 1918 would be worth about $125,000 in 2024. She was cremated and remains interned in the Woodlawn cemetery in NYC along with Emily Hanley, a teacher she taught with, in the plot owned by Grace M. Barns, another teacher.

Oscar E. Snyder was born five years later, in January of 1842 in NYC.

On Sept 5th, 1861, Oscar enlisted in company D, 6th regiment of the Connecticut Volunteer infantry at the age of 20. He reenlisted again in December 1863 in Hilton Head, NC. On June 17, 1864, Oscar was reported Missing-in-Action from Bermuda Hundred VA. Oscar had been captured by the south and was placed in a railroad train to be imprisoned at Andersonville, NC. Andersonville was a notorious prison where 1 in 4 men died. In a one-year period over 10,000 Union prisoners died. Oscar managed to jump off the train in route to Andersonville. He floated down the Ogeechee River in Georgia by night and laid in the swamps during the day. He was then recaptured. After his release from prison, at the end of the war, he was hospitalized December 1864 in Annapolis, MD and diagnosed with Typhoid Fever. He was not discharged from military service until August 1865 because of his lengthy illness. When he returned home to Round Hill his father referred to him as a walking skeleton.

Recovering from the Civil War, Oscar learned a trade as a dentist, most likely working with his dad. On Nov. 9, 1867, Oscar married Mary Fox in Stamford, CT. The wedding was at the bride's parent's home in Stamford. She grew up in North Stamford so they may have known each other before the war. The city of Stamford is next to the city of Greenwich. Mary was 28 years old and two years older than Oscar.

Oscar practiced dentistry in different cities including New York City, Chicago, and one year in Grand Rapids, MI. At some time, Oscar was president of the New England Dental Association. We know that Oscar was in a dental partnership with Wm. McChesney in Chicago around 1871 (the year of Mrs. O'Leary's fire). In NYC, his office was kitty-corner from his father and in competition. In Chicago, he installed Goodyear Dentures and was involved in a lawsuit by Goodyear which involved dentists all across the country. He suffered greatly from rheumatoid arthritis which he had ever since his time in the Civil War. He was planning to move to Denver but decided to move to Mexico where doctors said the warmer, drier climate would help his arthritis. He lived in Santa Fe, NM, in 1881. Then he headed south again. On January 21, 1882, Oscar died in Socorro, New Mexico. His cause of death was given as rheumatoid arthritis contracted around the heart. He died before his 40th birthday.

Oscar was buried in Stamford CT. His headstone inscription is "and Jesus said I am the resurrection and the life" (Newfield Cemetery). Mary (Fox) Snyder was buried in Fresh Pond, Long Island, NY. They had no children. We have no pictures of Oscar but believe he was over 6 feet tall.

Washington Irving Snyder arrived two years behind Oscar in May of 1844. Washington went by the name W. Irving Snyder.

Andrew Peck and Irving Snyder started the Peck & Snyder Sporting Goods company in 1866. The business was located at 124-128 Nassau Street in New York. They found early success with their invention of the first rubber-soled and canvas tennis shoe as well as the two-wheeled inline skates.

In order to promote baseball to a worldwide audience, Irving Snyder joined Chicago sporting goods owner and ex-baseball pitcher A.G. Spalding on a world tour in 1888. According to biographer Mark Lamster in his book "Spalding's World Tour," Irving had a secondary motive for the trip. He wanted to find an international buyer for thirty thousand pairs of roller-skates. They went to Australia, Egypt, England, France, Hawaii, Italy, and New Zealand. Several prominent baseball players of the time accompanied them. Snyder and Spalding's trip was designed to introduce baseball to a global market.

Irving married Mary A. Simpson on August 16, 1866, in Yoro, Honduras. They had five children during their marriage. He died on July 28, 1914, in New Castle, New York, at the age of 70, and was buried in Long Branch, New Jersey. At one time he owned the "Norwood" Hotel in Long Branch. After selling out the Peck & Snyder company to A.G. Spaulding in 1893 Irving still sold fishing tackle and ice skates in NYC before moving to Long Branch.

His closest relatives include Audrey Baston and her niece Nancy Drennen (3C 1x).

Ida Frances Snyder was the first child to be born in Round Hill, Greenwich, CT. in April 16, 1848. Ida was a schoolteacher and once taught in a two-room school with her sister Florence. Florence lived with Ida before Florence married. Ida was married twice. First to Luscious Green with whom she had one child, Olive (also a teacher). Her second marriage was to Joseph Lockwood, and they had no children. Her entire life appears to have been spent in the Greenwich, Cos Cob area of Connecticut. Ida died in 1914 and is buried in the Putnam cemetery in Greenwich.

Ward Beecher Snyder was born December 23rd, 1852, at Round Hill.

Ward started a sporting goods company that would compete with his brother W. Irving. Ward's catalog was only published in 1875, so the venture was short-lived. Ward then went into the steam engine business and small steam powered boats all in NYC. Ward manufactured and sold the "Little Giant" steam engine. Steam engines were used to power most manufacturing equipment with overhead pulleys, belts and drive shafts. He married Winiford Carroll and had a son, Arthur. After a separation, he would marry Mary Applegate, and they would have five children. Ward resided in Perth Amboy, NJ which is a short water commute to NYC. There are relatives from Ward in Surf City, NC and California.

Cornelia Johnson Snyder was born at Round Hill, Greenwich, Connecticut in January 1850. My Great Grandmother, see chapter 14 for a complete biography.

Florence Comstock Snyder was born July 1858 at Round Hill.

An interesting thing about Florence was her name. Florence was always considered a male name until the time of Florence Nightingale. In several census records when she was a child the census taker listed her as a male. She was also called Frank as a child.

After Florence attended a teacher's college in New York City, she became a schoolteacher. She worked in both Round Hill, Greenwich and the Cos Cob areas of New York prior to getting married. Later, Florence began working a job as a bookkeeper at Mianus Motorworks in Mianus, CT.

Florence appears to be unlucky in marriage. First, she married a man with the last name of Ferris. We know nothing of that marriage, but we know that Mr. Ferris died sometime before April 13, 1894, because on that date, Florence Ferris married George W. Gray in Stamford, Connecticut.

George was quite successful and served as the president of Mianus Motorworks where Florence worked. During their marriage, Florence made a most unfortunate decision when she took in a younger woman as a boarder. The younger woman was 31 when Florence was 48. This boarder soon became a friend. But, in a tragic twist of fate, George ended up leaving Florence for the younger woman!

Florence had some court actions against George surrounding their divorce. Newspapers indicated she could receive upwards of $100,000. Later, it was reported she received $60,000. $60,000 in 1910 has the equivalent of 2 million in buying power in 2024.

One relative said George was from Perth Amboy, NJ and that they made the Gray Marine engine. There was a George Gray in Perth Amboy in 1930 who was in ship building business, however our George Gray had nothing to do with the Gray Marine engine.

In the 1920's George Gray's brother Frank, who was from Detroit, would visit Florence and the family in Battle Creek. Frank's son Paul was about the same age as George and Robert Harris, Florence's nephews whom she lived with.

The story has it that Florence was fairly well off financially, that is until the market crash of 1929. Florence lived to 86 years old and is buried in Battle Creek in what was, until recently, an unmarked grave. The plot was owned by Joseph Harris, husband of her niece Ada. She is buried alongside her sister Cornelia. She was a member and supporter of the Congregational Church in Battle Creek.

Jennifer Snyder was born 1859 at White Plains, NY.

Jennifer moved to Brooklyn, New York with her mother when she was 16. We have no other record of what happened to her and believe she lived into her 30s.

Lotti L. Snyder was born May 1862 at Round Hill.

Lotti moved to Brooklyn, New York with her mother when she was 13. She married Benjamin Franklin Finney when she was 23 years old. Benjamin was a butcher in Greenwich, and they were married in NYC where W. Irving, her brother lived. She died before her second anniversary and is buried in the Round Hill Methodist cemetery.

Chapter 18

The Threads of Baseball and Enterprise: Our Link to Peck & Snyder

For us, the name "Peck & Snyder" isn't just a historical footnote. It's a tangible link to our ancestor, George Harris (1910-1985), and a vibrant piece of his family's story. George's life was deeply intertwined with his grandmother, Cornelia Snyder, who shared his home from his birth until he was 29. And it's through Cornelia that the connection to this renowned sporting goods company emerges.

Family lore whispers of Cornelia, as a young woman in bustling New York City, meticulously tying baseballs for Peck & Snyder. This wasn't just any company; in the 1870s and 1880s, Peck & Snyder reigned as the world's largest manufacturer and seller of sporting goods. But the connection runs deeper. Cornelia's brother, W. Irving Snyder, was the very "Snyder" of "Peck & Snyder."

The company's origins are as colorful as the era itself. Andrew Peck, a Civil War veteran and enterprising salesman, laid the foundation in 1866. Starting with humble beginnings, selling tops, games, and early baseball equipment on Nassau Street, Peck's ingenuity led him to create his own games, even selling them to the legendary P.T. Barnum. He began crafting baseballs in a small room at 109 Nassau Street, and soon partnered with Mr. Snyder, forming the iconic Peck & Snyder.

Their business flourished, moving to larger premises at 126 Nassau Street, eventually expanding to 126-128-130 Nassau. This six-story brick edifice, now lost to time, stood a mere eighth of a mile north of the New York Stock Exchange. Peck & Snyder was a powerhouse, offering a vast array of sporting equipment, games, uniforms, and even firefighting gear. Their annual catalogs, and specialized seasonal editions, became treasure troves of the era's sporting culture.

In 1894, A.G. Spalding acquired Peck & Snyder, but the name lived on, most notably with their celebrated American Club ice skates. Even after the sale, the entrepreneurial spirit remained in the Snyder family. Both W. Irving and his brother Ward established fishing tackle shops in New York City in the early 1900s.

The legacy of Peck & Snyder extends beyond business. Their commitment to preserving sporting history is evident in the 35 items they donated to the Smithsonian in the 1880s. Today, we can glimpse into their past through reprinted catalogs, such as the 1886 edition by Payne Press, and original catalogs held in the Library of Congress.

For our family, Peck & Snyder isn't just a company name. It's a thread woven into the fabric of our history, connecting us to a time of innovation, enterprise, and the very beginnings of organized American sports. It's a story of Cornelia's nimble fingers tying baseballs, of W. Irving's vision, and of the entrepreneurial spirit that shaped our ancestors' lives.

BASE-BALLS.

We take pleasure in offering to ball players our Wholesale Reduced Prices on Base-Balls. We have made a lasting reputation on these goods by keeping the quality *superior* to any in the market. The growing popularity of our

is owing to the uniform manner in which every Ball is made. We would caution players against many imitations that are offered. All of our brand are stamped as shown in the cut. Samples by mail, post paid. $1.75 each.

			Per doz.
Professional Dead Red Ball			$13 00
" " White Ball			15 00
Van Horn's " "			15 00
Harvey Ross " "			15 00
Ryan's " "			15 00
Peck & Snyder's Bounding Rock, lively			12 00
" " Atlantic, lively			12 00
" " Star Ball			9 00
" " New York Regulation, lively			9 00

REGULATION BASE-BALL BATS.

Our assortment of the above is the largest in the country. Clubs in ordering selected bats from the following styles, can depend on getting the best in the market. In ordering order by numbers. Also state what lengths are required. Men's, or Regulation Bats are 36, 38, or 40 inches long. Boys' Bats are from 24 to 34 inches long.

Per doz.

No. 100. Hill's Patent Spring Bat.
Made of second growth ash, tough and durable 9 00

No. 101. Hill's Patent Fluted Bat.
American willow, light and strong 6 00

No. 102. Willow Bat, Full Polished.
Imitation English willow, full French polished 8 00

No. 103. Half Polished Bat.
Same as 102, only half French polished 5 00

No. 105. Peck & Snyder's Wound Handle Bat.
Sapling ash, with handles wound round with cord and waxed. Very strong and durable 6 00

MUTUAL B.B.C. MODEL.

No. 106. Ash, Bass, Spruce, Pine & White Wood Bats.
Our Boston and Mutual model ash bats, free of blemish.. 3 50

Figure 9. Two pages from the 1873 Peck & Snyder catalog. Peck & Snyder had a patent on the "Professional Dead Ball" dated August 30, 1870. In the 1873 catalog, they offered the Professional Dead Ball, the Bounding Rock (lively), the Atlantic (lively), the Star Ball and the New York Regulation (lively) all of which they manufactured.

Chapter 19

Kirk Reunion

Eliza (Brown) Snyder's oldest sister was Julia (Brown) Kirk. She was about five years older than Eliza. She married James Kirk, and they moved to Hartland Michigan where they homesteaded 160 acres between ¼ and ½ mile due east of town. They were married in 1836 in Greenwich and lived there until moving to Michigan in 1847. Six of their nine children were born at Round Hill.

Julia passed away in 1855 at age 45 leaving nine children from 2 ½ years to 19. The story is they started the reunions on their mother's birthday several years after her death and the Civil war had passed. They had reunions every year for over 100 years. They did change the date to a more convent summer date.

Julia would be my 3 great aunts. I first learned of our relatives in the Howell, Hartland, Brighton, and Tyrone area from an autograph book that belonged to my Grandmother Ada Clark. Ada died before I was even born and her husband Joe, kept the autograph book as a memento of Ada.

In the 3" x 5" book were perhaps twenty pages signed by aunts, uncles, and cousins. In 1887 or 1888 when she was 16 years old. I had no idea who these people were and no one else did, although my uncle (Robert Harris) remembers going to a family gathering when he was a child. Turns out the aunts and uncles were Ada's mother's aunts and uncles, not hers.

Newspapers would often announce the gathering of the Kirk reunion. In August of 1924, it was the 56th reunion. That would indicate they started in 1868 shortly after the Civil War. At least three of the Kirk children had married and it was time to get together as they were moving from home. Two of the Kirk boys were married the year the reunions started. The 1925 reunion was to be held at the home of Fred and Hazel Preston. Hazel was a granddaughter of John and Julia, and they were living in the original homestead house. They were still at that residence in the late 1970s and there is a placard in the front yard designating it as a centennial farm.

At the Kirk reunion, a sign-in book was used every year. In 1978 when my family (David Harris) and uncle (Robert Harris) attended. It was interesting to page back through the attendance book and see what years other of our relatives had attended. We found a year when my uncle came with his mother and Grandmother Cornelia and Aunt Florence Gray.

We know that Eliza (Julia's sister) was there in 1882 from the signed document of Oscar Snyder's Civil War Pension records. In 1887 and 1888 Ada and her mother and sister Elizabeth attended, traveling by train from Chicago.

1924: 56th at John Kirk's in Howell, nearly 100 were present.

1925: At Kirk homestead, Fred Preston's

1926: 58th at Joseph Beebe's in Fenton, 80 present.

1927: Rev. C.H. Rayl and the family, of Huntington, West Virginia attended the Kirk reunion. Mrs. Rayl was formerly Bessie Kirk.

The following is a copy of the Kirk Family as they had their reunions:

John Kirk Family from Livingston Co. Michigan

James Kirk Sr. was the eldest son of a family of wealth, sent on a voyage around the world. In New York, he met and married Mary Putnam, sister of General Putnam of Connecticut Revolutionary War fame. His wife was disowned by her people as she sided with her brother and her husband who were rebels, and the others in the family were Tories and loyal to England. James Kirk never returned to England to claim an estate left to him by his father. James Kirk and Rebecca had eleven children. He was a member of the street church or meeting house, for years weekday meetings for denominations were held at his house. Their third son, John, was born January 7, 1800.

John married Julia Brown, born 1810. Julia was one of three daughters of Nehemiah Brown Jr. of Round Hill, Conn. The others were Sarah and Jane. Their mother's first name was Elizabeth (the last name is unknown to this writer at this time). The Brown family was from England and came to America with the New Haven Colony. Very little is known of the origins of this family, though there is a record by Thomas Brown, a brother of Peter Brown, who was a signer of the New Haven Charter and went to live in Stamford, Conn., in a land grant on the border of New York, north of Long Island, by the Sovereign in 1660. John, born in 1680, and Samuel Jr. married the elder two daughters of the second son of Peter Brown and his wife. Roger Brown, born in 1726, received several hundred acres to the north of Round Hill. He was very active in the cause of the Revolution and held the rank of lieutenant. Nehemiah and Sophia had eleven children. Their home was the site of the present Round Hill Church and a travel road.

Nehemiah Brown Jr., the father of Julia (Brown) Kirk, was born in 1760 at Round Hill, Greenwich, Connecticut, the fourth son of Nehemiah Brown Sr. and his wife Sophia. He served in the Connecticut militia in the early years of the Revolutionary War, doing guard duty at Saw Pit (now Port Chester) and at Pound

Ridge on the border of Connecticut and New York. He was present at the retreat of the Continental Army under General Washington from New York City and later joined that army until the end of the war. He attained the rating of captain. On his death in 1840, he willed approximately fifty acres apiece to each of his three daughters at Round Hill. Sarah married a man with the last name of Ford. They lived in the area until the late 1870s. Jane married a dentist from New York—Dr. Wm. Snyder. They lived at Round Hill and White Plains, N.Y. They had ten children: one an artist, four schoolteachers. A son, Caesar, was a dentist and a musician. He served in the Civil War with the 6th Conn. Vol., was captured 12th of June 1864 and sent to Fort Sumter (Andersonville) prison in Georgia, where he was interned with his cousin Newton Thorn Kirk of the 26th Michigan Vol., captured 12th of May 1864. (Of the forty-five thousand Union soldiers confined there, over twelve thousand died, but both survived the ordeal.) Some of these cousins and their descendants attended the Kirk family reunions.

John and Julia sold their fifty acres in Connecticut for the sum of one hundred fifty dollars and moved to Michigan in the fall of 1847. Here they settled in Burns, Livingston Co., near Hartland. John cleared and improved 160 acres of land for their homestead. Julia died the 4th of September after giving birth to nine children: Newton Thorn, Nehemiah Brown, Julia Elizabeth, Albert, Emily, Arlington, Katherine Rebecca, Edward, and Frank. Julia Elizabeth married into the Beebe family, Emily into the Fraley family, and Katherine Rebecca into the Chamber family. From these and the Kirk boys with their spouses devolved the present-day Kirk generations who continue to celebrate the 60th birthday and a new housewarming for John Kirk which was started June 7th, 1869. We must honor with all due respect Emeline Wheaton, who consented to be the second wife of John in 1857 after the death of Julia, for without her help he would have had quite a problem raising the children, the youngest age five.

John Kirk died in 1893 at the age of eighty-three. Throughout the years, his family and the succeeding generations have made a substantial contribution to the communities around Hartland, Burns Township, Livingston Co., Michigan. Today, in 1982, there is only one person left with the family name of Kirk who is descended from John and Julia Kirk.

Interesting things about this Kirk Family account:

This account was written over 50 years ago by members of the Kirk family. It was written from Julia Brown family stories as handed down to them. It was acquired at a Kirk family reunion.

It shows Elizabeth as the mother of the three Brown girls (Julia, Sarah and Eliza). not Sarah Purdy.

My relatives, being descendants of Eliza, referred to her as Eliza Jane Brown. I have found no historical records with the middle name of Jane. Interestingly the Kirk family called her Jane.

The Kirk account states Nehemiah Brown attained the rank of Captain which I could not confirm through his military records, but his first marriage shows Capt. Nehemiah Brown married Sarah Purdy.

Chapter 20

Nehemiah Brown Jr.

Nehemiah Brown Jr. b. March 19, 1855 (or 1860) d. August 8, 1840

Nehemiah Brown Jr. was one of eight children born to Nehemiah Brown Sr. and Sophia Park in Round Hill, Greenwich, CT. Because he is a Jr., his birthday is more likely 1855 as that would make him the eldest son.

In the years before the revolutionary war (1775), each town had their own military called the "Train Band". They would meet monthly for military training and included all able-bodied men 16 and over. Nehemiah Jr. as well as his brother Major Brown would have been in the Greenwich "Train Band". Records show he served every year for short stints in Greenwich, CT. and Westchester County NY. throughout the Revolution.   As his many grandchildren grew up in the Round Hill area he would tell stories of his exploits during the revelation. His Revolutionary War record shows date of birth as 1760.

Nehemiah would have married Sarah Purdy when he was 42 and Sarah was 21. On September 3, 1797. Marriage may have been Aug 27th, 1797, as it was reported in the New York Weekly Museum (newspaper). Nehemiah and Sarah would live with Nehemiah's father. This house was located at the northwest corner of John St. and Buckfield Lane, in Round Hill. Sarah Purdy was the daughter of Nehemiah's cousin Caleb Purdy who died when Sarah was 7 years old. June 21, 1798, Nehemiah Brown Jr. and Sarah Brown (his wife) purchased 10 acres of land from Ruth Purdy (Sarah's mother). On April 11, 1799, Nehemiah lost his first wife Sarah after two years of marriage. She is buried next to Nehemiah's mother (Sophia Brown) in the Burning Hill Cemetery. She has a small hand etched stone that is difficult to find. The headstone reads S. P. B. 11 Apr 1799. There are no records for the death of Sarah Purdy Brown. In about 1808-1810, Nehemiah would marry Elizabeth (Betsy) at age 53+/- and she was 19+/-.

The Round Hill Methodist Episcopal church began in 1810 as people in the Round Hill area met in homes. In 1826, the first Church was built on the south side of John Street and a cemetery adjacent to it. It was later rebuilt and moved across the street to the North side. The cemetery remains. The membership record is only given as a group from 1810 to 1858. From church records of the Town of Greenwich pub. 1912 Spencer Mead, page 136. We find Betsy Brown, Nehemiah Brown, and Sarah Brown. This listing shows Nehemiah next to Sarah. This is also an alphabetical list, and Nehemiah would be next to Sarah alphabetically. Another source for these church records does not list them alphabetically and Betsy and Nehemiah are listed next to each other and Sarah is listed later. By this Sarah is most likely Sarah the daughter of Nehemiah. Nehemiah and his daughter Sarah Ford are buried in the Cemetery.

Nehemiah died at age 80 in 1840, Elizabeth was 34 yrs. younger, (46) at that time. In Nehemiah's will dated June 8, 1839, probated Aug. 22, 1840, mentioned his wife Elizabeth, and children Julia Kirk, Sarah Ford, and Eliza Snyder. The property was to be divided into 3rds however the land would not pass to the girls until the death of his wife Elizabeth (Betsie).

Betsie Brown died March 26, 1869, at the age of 79. She was born in Greenwich, and her parents were Susan and Minor (no last name).

Concerning Nehemiah's Ancestors.

In 1761 Nehemiah Sr. was authorized by the Connecticut General Assembly to keep a public house and "retail strong drink" (location unknown).

Among the first settlers was Samuel Brown II (1689-1750), the son of Samuel Brown of Rye, New York, who received a royal grant of 1000 acres there. Samuel II built the saltbox in the district on John Street. The house passed down to his eldest son, Samuel III. Since he also inherited the Rye property, he sold the Round Hill property in 1762 to his brother, Nehemiah, a tavern keeper and one of the principal farmers here. It is said that Nehemiah and his brother, Roger, eventually owned more than 700 acres in Greenwich. The house remained in the family well into the twentieth century, when it was sold for use as a parsonage by the Kenworthy family, who were related to the Browns by marriage. Roger sold his property and moved his family to Rising Sun, Indiana.

Chapter 21

Sarah Purdy - First Wife of Nehemiah Brown Jr.

Sarah Purdy b. 1776 married Nehemiah Brown 3 Sept 1897 in Greenwich. Nehemiah was 16 years older than Sarah. I believe she died two years after her marriage on 11 Apr 1899. She would be just 22 years old and had no children. She is buried in the Burying Hill cemetery near her mother-in-law.

Note: Most records showing Sarah Purdy as the mother of Julia, Sarah and Eliza come from family trees with no source records. Most genealogies on the internet have their roots in Ancestry.com The only sources being her birth and marriage record. From this everyone has assumed she was the mother of Julia, Sarah and Eliza, and we know what ASSUME stands for.

Following the Purdy lineage:

Caleb Purdy 1711 -1794 Rye, NY m. Hannah Brown 1721 – 1805

    Caleb Purdy 1743 – 1783 Rye, NY m. Ruth Peck 1746 - 1822

        Sarah Purdy (Brown) b. 1776 d. 1799? m. 1797

        Ruth Purdy b. 1772 d. 1845 m. Nathaniel Knapp

        Caleb b. 1774 d. 1795 m. Mary Reynolds

        Elias b. 1780 d. 1828 m Clara Peck

Chapter 22

Betsy (Elizabeth) - Second Wife of Nehemiah Brown Jr.

Betsy or Elizabeth was born in 1790 in Connecticut, her parents were Minor and Susan and their last name unknown. She died at the age of 79 while living at Round Hill on March 28, 1869. Her burial location is unknown, but she is likely buried next to Nehemiah Brown, in an unmarked grave, at the M. E. Church cemetery at Round.

The first record of Elizabeth is found in the will of Nehemiah Brown dated June 8, 1839, Greenwich. Elizabeth was to receive all of Nehemiah's real and personal property for all of her natural life. After her death the property was to be divided into 1/3's for Julia, Sarah and Eliza. From census records she would have been born between 1790 and 1794 in Connecticut.

A genealogy record of the Kirk Family (Julia) in Michigan, written over 50 years ago lists Elizabeth as the mother of Julia, not Sarah.

1850 census Elizabeth Brihn (Brown) age 56 b. CT head of house. Living with her was Wm. Snidyer 32, Eliza 33, Wil 12, Oscar 12, Irving 8, Ida 2 and Ever 5/12 (March)

1853, Aug 24 Betsy Brown is paid $100 for purchase of William Snyder's furniture and utensils which were in the house they were living in together. Sometime after this (1858?) Wm and Eliza moved to White plains as that is where they were in the 1860 census.

1855 agriculture census Elizabeth Brown is shown next to Major Brown with 36 acres. The agriculture census does not list occupants.

1857 Map of Greenwich shows Snyder on St. Johns Street just west of Buckfield Ln. which is the location of Elizabth Brown.

1860 census Betsy Brown, living at Round Hill (next to Major Brown) age 69, estate $2500 and personal value $100. Living with her is James Sanders (London, Souden?) family (wife and five children) to do farm labor. James' oldest son, David, is living with Major Brown.

1867 land map of Greenwich shows Dr. Snyder home at the north end of Buckfield Ln. This is the most likely location for the homestead painting by Wilhelmina.

Round Hill M.E. church started in 1810, but membership record only list those who were members between 1810 and 1858. Members include Nehemiah Brown, Sarah Brown (daughter) and Betsy Brown. From a search we know that Betsy and Nehemiah joined together.

On 3/2/1880 Eliza sells 50 acres of land she inherited from Nehemiah to W. Irving Snyder. Around 1891 Irving's siblings sign off on the purchase of the land as the original will left the land to Eliza, for her lifetime and then to her children.

Perhaps part of the rift that occurred between Wm. & Eliza Snyder may have stemmed from the relationship with Betsy? Or maybe the way in which Wm. Bought and sold land when he was obviously left out of Nehemiah's will.

Chapter 23

Descendants of Nehemiah Brown Jr.

Pedigree Chart for
Nehemiah (Jr) Brown

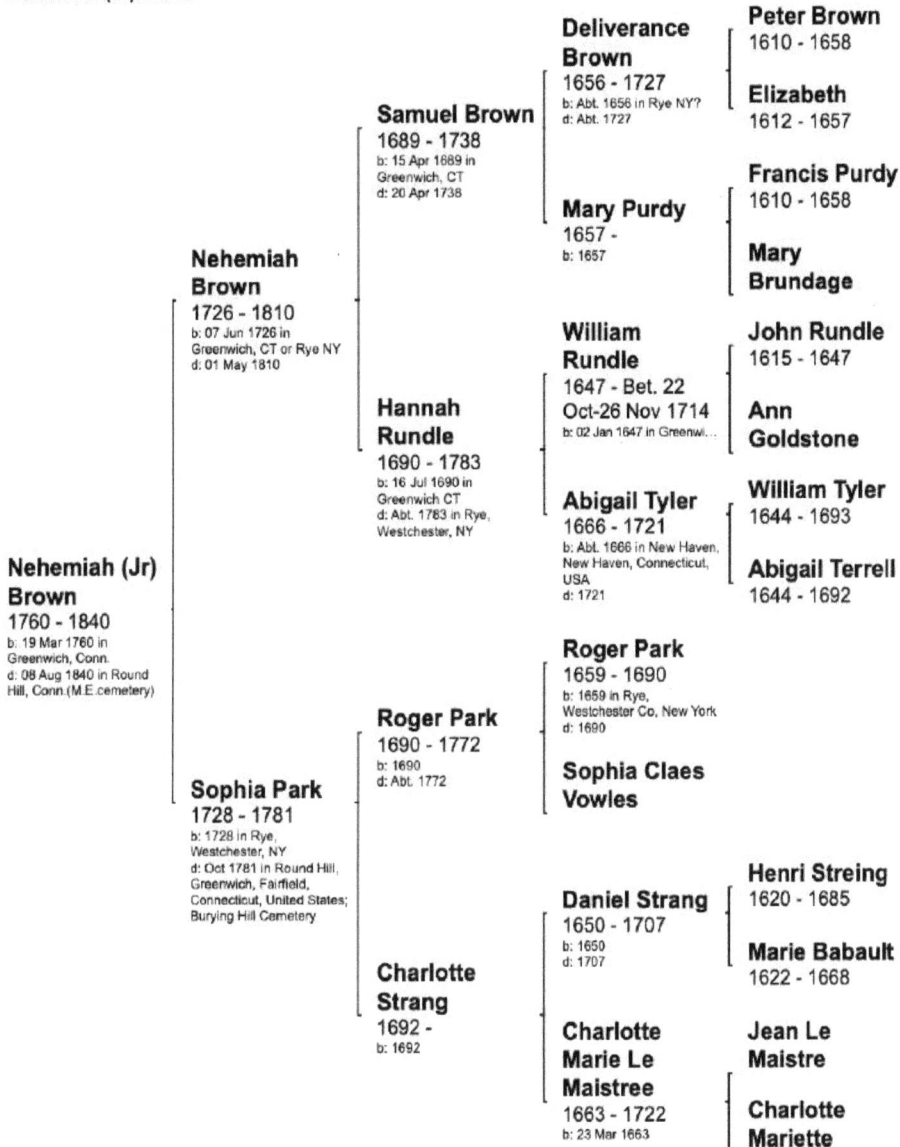

Nehemiah (Jr) Brown
1760 - 1840
b: 19 Mar 1760 in
Greenwich, Conn.
d: 08 Aug 1840 in Round
Hill, Conn.(M.E.cemetery)

Nehemiah Brown
1726 - 1810
b: 07 Jun 1726 in
Greenwich, CT or Rye NY
d: 01 May 1810

Sophia Park
1728 - 1781
b: 1728 in Rye,
Westchester, NY
d: Oct 1781 in Round Hill,
Greenwich, Fairfield,
Connecticut, United States;
Burying Hill Cemetery

Samuel Brown
1689 - 1738
b: 15 Apr 1689 in
Greenwich, CT
d: 20 Apr 1738

Hannah Rundle
1690 - 1783
b: 16 Jul 1690 in
Greenwich CT
d: Abt. 1783 in Rye,
Westchester, NY

Roger Park
1690 - 1772
b: 1690
d: Abt. 1772

Charlotte Strang
1692 -
b: 1692

Deliverance Brown
1656 - 1727
b: Abt. 1656 in Rye NY?
d: Abt. 1727

Mary Purdy
1657 -
b: 1657

William Rundle
1647 - Bet. 22 Oct-26 Nov 1714
b: 02 Jan 1647 in Greenwi...

Abigail Tyler
1666 - 1721
b: Abt. 1666 in New Haven,
New Haven, Connecticut,
USA
d: 1721

Roger Park
1659 - 1690
b: 1659 in Rye,
Westchester Co, New York
d: 1690

Sophia Claes Vowles

Daniel Strang
1650 - 1707
b: 1650
d: 1707

Charlotte Marie Le Maistree
1663 - 1722
b: 23 Mar 1663

Peter Brown
1610 - 1658

Elizabeth
1612 - 1657

Francis Purdy
1610 - 1658

Mary Brundage

John Rundle
1615 - 1647

Ann Goldstone

William Tyler
1644 - 1693

Abigail Terrell
1644 - 1692

Henri Streing
1620 - 1685

Marie Babault
1622 - 1668

Jean Le Maistre

Charlotte Mariette

Descendants of Nehemiah (Jr) Brown

1.   **NEHEMIAH (JR) BROWN** was born on 19 Mar 1760 in Greenwich, CT. He died on 08 Aug 1840 in Round Hill, CT. (M.E. cemetery). He married (1) **SARAH PURDY**, daughter of Caleb Purdy and Ruth Peck on 03 Sep 1797 in Greenwich, CT. She was born on 16 Jun 1776 in Greenwich (Barbour collection). She died on 11 Apr 1799 (Burying Hill cemetery Round Hill). He married **ELIZABETH**. She was born in 1790 in Greenwich CT. She died on 26 Mar 1869 in Greenwich CT (Page 478).

   Nehemiah (Jr) Brown and Sarah Purdy had the following children:

2.   i. JULIA BROWN was born on 10 July 1810 in Round Hill, CT. She died on 04 Sep 1855 in Hartland, Livingston Co. MI. She married John B. Kirk, son of James Kirk and Rebecca B. Chevvis on 04 July 1836 in NYC Methodist Church Records. He was born on 07 Jan 1809 in Ct or NY. He died on 17 Jun 1893 in Hartland, Livingston Co. MI.

   ii. SARAH P. BROWN was born in 1812 in Round Hill, Greenwich, Connecticut, United States. She died on 09 May 1874 in Manhattan, New York City, New York, United States. She married Henry H. Ford before 1840. He died before 1873.

3.   iii. ELIZA JANE BROWN was born on 28 Mar 1815 in Round Hill, Greenwich, Connecticut, United States. She died on 22 Mar 1900 in Chicago, Cook Co., IL. She married William D. Snyder, son of William Snyder and Phebe Owen on 11 Feb 1837 in Methodist Episcopal Church, NYC. He was born in 1818 in Dutchess Co., NY? (marriage of Ida). He died on 17 Mar 1894 in Stamford, CT (Stamford newspaper April 7, 1894).

Generation 2

2.   **JULIA BROWN** (Nehemiah (Jr)) was born on 10 July 1810 in Round Hill, CT. She died on 04 Sep 1855 in Hartland, Livingston Co. MI. She married John B. Kirk, son of James Kirk and Rebecca B. Chevvis on 04 Jul 1836 in NYC Methodist Church Records. He was born on 07 Jan 1809 in CT or NY. He died on 17 Jun 1893 in Hartland, Livingston Co. MI.

   Julia Brown and John B. Kirk had the following children:

4.   i. NEWTON THORN KIRK was born on 15 Apr 1836 in Greenwich, CT. He died on 19 Sep 1909 in Los Angeles, CA. He married Mary Electra Walcott on 29 Sep 1868 in Burns, Michigan. She was born on 18 Nov 1841 in Burns, Michigan. She died date Unknown.

5.   ii. NEHEMIAH B. KIRK was born in 1838 in Fairfield, CT. He died on 22 Dec 1895 in Howell, Michigan. He married Clarissa Haines on 07 Oct 1868. She was born about 1842 in Michigan.

6.   iii.   JULIA ELIZABETH KIRK was born on 10 Feb 1840 in Fairfield, CT. She died on 10 May 1915 in Highland Park, Wayne, Michigan, United States. She married (1) DANIEL BEEBE on 20 Sep 1856 in Livingston Co. Michigan. He was born in Oct 1835. He died on 24 Oct 1865 in Livingston Co. MI (Riddle cem). She married (2) AMOS BEEBE in Mar 1867. He was born about 1828. He died in 1915.

7.   iv.   ALBERT KIRK was born on 20 Jan 1842 in Greenwich, CT. He died on 01 Jan 1908 in Fenton, Michigan. He married ELEANOR WHALEN. She was born date Unknown. She died date Unknown. He married CYNTHIA A. HORTON.

8.   v.   EMILY F. KIRK was born on 24 Feb 1844 in Ct. She died on 15 Apr 1929 in Tyrone, Livingston, Michigan, USA. She married Charles B. Marvin on 05 Oct 1864. He was born on 13 June 1843.

9.   vi.   ARLINGTON KIRK was born on 15 Oct 1846 in Round Hill, CT. He died on 07 Jun 1918 in Hartland, Livingston Co. MI. He married (1) FRANCES MILDRED ADAMS on 18 Dec 1872. She was born in May 1850. She died on 01 Jun 1882 in Livingston Co. MI (Riddle cem). He married (2) MARY EDWINA BURDICK on 30 Nov 1887 in Howell, Michigan. She was born about 1862. She died on 28 Mar 1935 in Hartland, Livingston Co. MI.

10.   vii.   KATHERINE REBECCA KIRK was born on 31 Oct 1847 in Michigan. She died in 1920 in Illinois (HC). She married Zabina Everett Chambers date Unknown. He was born about 1849. He died in 1913 in Hartland, Livingston Co. MI.

11.   viii.   EDWARD KIRK was born on 07 Oct 1850 in Michigan. He died on 15 Feb 1933 in Hartland, Livingston Co. MI. He married Harriet (Hattie) Ada Alverson on 05 Jan 1875 in Howell, MI. She was born in 1854. She died on 22 Jun 1925 in Hartland, Livingston Co. MI.

12.   ix.   FRANK P. KIRK was born on 02 Dec 1852 in Michigan. He died on 14 Jan 1900 in Tyrone, Livingston, MI. He married Melissa Deal on 20 Dec 1876 in Hartland, Livingston Co. MI.

3.   **ELIZA JANE BROWN** (Nehemiah (Jr) was born on 28 Mar 1815 in Round Hill, Greenwich, Connecticut, United States. She died on 22 Mar 1900 in Chicago, Cook Co., IL. She married William D. Snyder, son of William Snyder and Phebe Owen on 11 Feb 1837 in Methodist Episcopal Church, NYC. He was born in 1818 in Dutchess Co., NY? (marriage of Ida). He died on 17 Mar 1894 in Stamford, CT (Stamford newspaper April 7, 1894).

Eliza Jane Brown and William D. Snyder had the following children:

i.   WILHELMINA SNYDER was born on 12 Jan 1838 in New York City. She died on 28 June 1918 in Battle Creek, MI (Woodlawn cem, NYC).

ii. OSCAR E. SNYDER was born in 1842 in New York City. He died on 21 Jan 1882 in Socorro, New Mexico. He married Mary E. Fox, daughter of Ellsworth Fox and Phobe Cook on 09 Oct 1867 in Stamford, CT. She was born in 1839 in Stamford, CT. She died on 01 Jan 1923 in N.Y.C.

13.   iii.   WASHINGTON IRVING SNYDER was born in May 1844 in New York City. He died on 28 July 1914 in New Castle NY (Glenwood cem. Long Branch, NJ). He married Mary Ann Simpson, daughter of Richard Simpson on 16 Aug 1866 in Brooklyn, Kings, NY. She was born on 25 Apr 1846 in NY. She died on 11 May 1914 in Long Branch, NJ (Glenwood Cem.).

14.   iv.   IDA FRANCES SNYDER was born on 16 Apr 1848 in Round Hill, Greenwich, CT. She died on 08 Sep 1914 in Greenwich, Conn. (Putnam cemetery, Greenwich). She married LUSIOUS GREEN. She married (2) JOSEPH ALBERT LOCKWOOD on 18 Jul 1888 in Greenwich, CT. He was born on 08 July 1843 in CT. He died in 1922.

15.   v.   CORNELIA JOHNSON SNYDER was born on 12 Jan 1850 in Round Hill, Greenwich, CT. She died on 07 Feb 1940 in Battle Creek, MI. She married James M. Clark, son of Chauncy H. Clark and Mary C. Corwin on 27 Dec 1871 in Greenwich, CT. He was born on 29 Jan 1851 in Middletown, Orange, NY. He died on 06 Aug 1922 in Tulsa, OK.

16.   vi.   WARD BEECHER SNYDER was born on 23 Dec 1852 in Round Hill, Greenwich, CT. He died on 29 Oct 1916 in Madison NJ (Christ Church Cemetery, South Amboy, NJ). He married (1) MARY B. APPLEGATE, daughter of Charles Applegate and Mary Morse in 1878. She was born on 15 Dec 1857 in South Amboy (Middlesex) NJ. She died on 30 Dec 1944 in Glenridge, (Essex) NJ (Christ Church Cemetery, South Amboy, NJ). He married (2) WINIFORD CARROLL on 17 Jan 1874 in Manhattan, NYC. She was born in June 1855. She died in 1915.

   vii.   FLORENCE COMSTOCK SNYDER was born about 23 July 1858 in Round Hill, CT. She died on 11 Mar 1935 in Battle Creek, MI. She married (1) FREDRICK M. FERRIS after 1884. She married (2) GEORGE W. GRAY, son of Amander W. Gray and Frances Peckhouse on 18 Apr 1894 in Greenwich, CT. He was born on 12 Aug 1863 in CT. He died on 20 Dec 1920 in Ledyard, New London, Connecticut, USA.

   viii.   JENNIFER SNYDER was born in 1859 in White plains, NY. She died after 1891.

   ix.   LOTTI L. SNYDER was born on 15 May 1862 in White Plains, NY. She died on 28 Sep 1886 in Greenwich, CT. (Round Hill M.E. cemetery). She married Benjamin Franklin Finney on 24 Oct 1884 in Manhattan, NYC.

Generation 3

4. **NEWTON THORN KIRK** (Julia Brown, Nehemiah (Jr)) was born on 15 Apr 1836 in Greenwich, CT. He died on 19 Sep 1909 in Los Angeles, CA. He married Mary Electra Walcott on 29 Sep 1868 in Burns, MI. She was born on 18 Nov 1841 in Burns, MI..
    Newton Thorn Kirk and Mary Electra Walcott had the following children:
    i. LILIAN KIRK was born in 1869. She died on 15 Sep 1928 in Grand Rapids, MI. She married Edward A. Armstrong on 11 Nov 1891 in Albion, MI. He was born on 11 Feb 1869 in Almont, Lapeer, MI. He died on 17 Mar 1953.
    ii. JANE E. KIRK was born on 13 Jun 1874. She married William L. Barth on 07 Sep 1898 in Albion, MI. He was born in 1862.

5. **NEHEMIAH B. KIRK** (Julia Brown, Nehemiah (Jr)) was born in 1838 in Fairfield, CT. He died on 22 Dec 1895 in Howell, Michigan. He married Clarissa Haines on 07 Oct 1868. She was born about 1842 in Michigan. She died date Unknown.
    Nehemiah B. Kirk and Clarissa Haines had the following child:
    i. JOHN KIRK was born about 1871 in Michigan.

6. **JULIA ELIZABETH (Libb) KIRK** (Julia$_2$ Brown, Nehemiah (Jr)$_1$) was born on 10 Feb 1840 in Fairfield, CT. She died on 10 May 1915 in Highland Park, Wayne, MI. She married (1) **DANIEL BEEBE** on 20 Sep 1856 in Livingston Co. MI. He was born in Oct 1835. He died on 24 Oct 1865 in Livingston Co. MI (Riddle cem). She married (2) **AMOS BEEBE** in Mar 1867. He was born in 1828. He died 1915.
    Julia Elizabeth Kirk and Daniel Beebe had the following children:
    i. JULIA ADELLE BEEBE was born on 25 July 1859 in Oceola Township, Livingston, MI. She died on 17 Apr 1921 in Detroit, Wayne, MI. She married Charles Edward Kellogg on 11 Nov 1880 in Howell, Livingston, Mi. He was born on 04 Sep 1858 in Oceola Township, Livingston, MI. He died on 04 Apr 1910 in Detroit, Wayne, MI.
    ii. JOSEPH F. BEEBE. He died in 1944.
    Julia Elizabeth Kirk and Amos Beebe had the following children:
    i. JOSEPH FRANKLIN BEEBE was born on 02 Aug 1869. He died on 29 Jul 1944. He married Bertha Van Tiffin about 1897. She was born about 1874.
    ii. BERTHA J. BEEBE was born on 06 Jul 1875. She married Irwin A. Root in 1908.

7. **ALBERT KIRK** (Julia Brown, Nehemiah (Jr)) was born on 20 Jan 1842 in Greenwich, CT. He died on 01 Jan 1908 in Fenton, Michigan. He married **ELEANOR WHALEN**. She was born date Unknown. She died date Unknown. He married (2) **CYNTHIA A. HORTON**.
    Albert Kirk and Cynthia A. Horton had the following children:
    i. IDA KIRK was born in 1868.
    ii. JULIA B. KIRK was born in 1871.

iii.   NETTIE R was born on 31 Jan 1876 in Livingston Co. MI. She died on 05 Apr 1951 in CA. She married FRANK MOORLAND. He was born in 1876.

8.   **EMILY F. KIRK** (Julia[2] Brown, Nehemiah (Jr)[1]) was born on 24 Feb 1844 in CT. She died on 15 Apr 1929 in Tyrone, Livingston, MI. She married Charles B. Marvin on 05 Oct 1864. He was born on 13 June 1843.

Emily F. Kirk and Charles B. Marvin had the following children:

i.   JULIA R. MARVIN was born on 11 Sep 1880 in Tyrone twp., Livingston Co., MI. She died in (never Married).

ii.   JOHN R. MARVIN was born on 28 Mar 1871 in Hartland, MI. He married KATE B. WARNER. She was born in Oct 1871 in Michigan.

iii.   METTA N. MARVIN was born on 15 Feb 1868 in Hartland, MI. She died in 1938. She married George S Lawrence on 07 Aug 1906. He was born about 1878 in Vermont.

iv.   WILLIAM EDWARD MARVIN was born on 07 Aug 1865 in Hartland, MI.

v.   MAUD MARVIN was born on 16 Jun 1869 in Hartland, MI.

vi.   FREDRICK MARVIN was born on 07 Sep 1874 in Hartland, MI. He married ADDIE A. JARRARD. She was born in Feb 1878 in Ohio.

9.   **ARLINGTON KIRK** (Julia[2] Brown, Nehemiah (Jr)[1]) was born on 15 Oct 1846 in Round Hill, CT. He died on 07 Jun 1918 in Hartland, Livingston Co. MI. He married (1) **FRANCES MILDRED ADAMS** on 18 Dec 1872. She was born in May 1850. She died on 01 Jun 1882 in Livingston Co. MI (Riddle cem). He married (2) **MARY EDWINA BURDICK** on 30 Nov 1887 in Howell, MI. She was born about 1862. She died on 28 Mar 1935 in Hartland, Livingston Co. MI.

Arlington Kirk and Frances Mildred Adams had the following children:

i.   LIZZIE MILLARD KIRK was born on 11 Dec 1879 in Livingston Co. MI. She died on 02 Sep 1880 in Livingston Co. MI (Riddle cem).

ii.   LOUIS A. KIRK was born in 1878. He married BELLE. She was born about 1885.

Arlington Kirk and Mary Edwina Burdick had the following children:

iii.   HAZEL KIRK was born on 07 Oct 1888. She died on 24 Mar 1982 in Hartland, Livingston Co. MI. She married FRED RAY PRESTON. He was born on 31 Jan 1887. He died on 17 July 1979 in Hartland, Livingston, MI

iv.   FRANCES (BESSIE) KIRK was born in 1892.

v.   ARLINGTON BURDICK KIRK was born on 18 Oct 1896 in Livingston, MI.

10.   **KATHERINE REBECCA KIRK** (Julia Brown, Nehemiah (Jr)) was born on 31 Oct 1847 in MI. She died in 1920 in Illinois. She married Zabina Everett Chambers. He was born about 1849. He died in 1913 in Hartland, Livingston Co. MI.

Katherine Rebecca Kirk and Zabina Everett Chambers had the following children:

i.   CHURCHILL L. CHAMBERS was born in 1880 in Michigan.

ii.   JULIA FRANCES CHAMBERS was born about 1870 in Michigan. She died on 12 Aug 1872 in Hartland, Livingston Co. MI.

iii.   MYRTLE E. CHAMBERS was born on 21 Mar 1874 in Michigan. She died on 23 Sep 1877 in Hartland, Livingston Co. MI.

iv.   SARAH A. was born in May 1883 in Hartland, Livingston, MI. She married WILLIAM G. STRUGGLES. He was born on 16 Mar 1876 in Pontiac, MI. He died on 10 Feb 1939 in Winnetka, Cook Co., IL.

11.   **EDWARD KIRK** (Julia Brown, Nehemiah (Jr)) was born on 07 Oct 1850 in MI. He died on 15 Feb 1933 in Hartland, Livingston Co. MI. He married Harriet (Hattie) Ada Alverson on 05 Jan 1875 in Howell, Michigan. She was born in 1854. She died on 22 Jun 1925 in Hartland, Livingston Co. MI.

Edward Kirk and Harriet (Hattie) Ada Alverson had the following children:

i.   JULIA M. KIRK was born on 08 Apr 1876. She died on 19 Sep 1877 in Hartland, Livingston Co. MI.

ii.   CORA A. KIRK was born in Jan 1879.

iii.   NORA A. KIRK was born in 1879.

iv.   ADA F. KIRK was born in Nov 1882. She died in 1922 in Hartland, Livingston Co. MI. She married MR CAMPBELL.

v.   HARLEY J. KIRK was born in Aug 1894. He died in 1920 in a sanitarium for TB.

12.   **FRANK P. KIRK** (Julia Brown, Nehemiah (Jr)) was born on 02 Dec 1852 in MI. He died on 14 Jan 1900 in Tyrone, Livingston, Michigan, USA. He married Melissa Deal on 20 Dec 1876 in Hartland, Livingston Co. MI..

Frank P. Kirk and Melissa Deal had the following child:

i. MYRTIA P. KIRK was born in 1881. She died in 1966. She married JUDSON COX.

13.   **WASHINGTON IRVING SNYDER** (Eliza Jane Brown, Nehemiah (Jr)) was born in May 1844 in New York City. He died on 28 July 1914 in New Castle NY (Glenwood cem. Long Branch, NJ). He married Mary Ann Simpson, daughter of Richard Simpson on 16 Aug 1866 in Brooklyn, Kings, NY. She was born on 25 Apr 1846 in NY. She died on 11 May 1914 in Long Branch, NJ (Glenwood Cem.).

Washington Irving Snyder and Mary Ann Simpson had the following children:

i.   EMMA SNYDER was born on 13 Oct 1867 in NY. She died in Feb 1950 in Mt Pleasant, NY. She married Frank Stutzer Eldredge on 14 Nov 1894 in New York City. He was born in Oct 1867. He died in 1935.

ii.   PERCY E. SNYDER was born in May 1868. He died on 01 Jan 1907 in Eighth Ave & 27 th. street. Saloon in N.Y.C.

iii.   ELIZABETH (LIZZIE) SNYDER was born about 1871 in New Jersey. She died in 1955. She married Ralph Wentworth Milne on 15 June 1897 in Brooklyn, Kings, NY. He was born in Aug 1871 in Pennsylvania. He died on 20 Sep 1949.

iv.   JESSIE KIRK SNYDER was born in Feb 1876 in NY (census). She died in 1942. She married Theodore Edward Belts on 09 Dec 1896 in N.Y.C. He was born on 23 Sep 1868 in Hornellsville, Steuben, New York, United States. He died after 1930.

v.   WARNER B. SNYDER was born on 11 Apr 1877. He died on 30 Dec 1914 in Long Branch, NJ.

14.   **IDA FRANCES SNYDER** (Eliza Jane Brown, Nehemiah (Jr)) was born on 16 Apr 1848 in Round Hill, Greenwich, Connecticut, United States. She died on 08 Sep 1914 in Greenwich, CT. (Putnam cemetery, Greenwich). She married **LUSIOUS GREEN**. She married (2) **JOSEPH ALBERT LOCKWOOD** on 18 Jul 1888 in Greenwich, CT. He was born on 08 Jul 1843 in Connecticut. He died in 1922.
Ida Frances Snyder and Lusious Green had the following child:

i.   OLIVE GREEN was born on 16 June 1875. She died in Dec 1936. She married John Sullivan on 26 Sep 1910 in Manhattan, NYC. He was born in 1882 in Ireland.

15.   **CORNELIA JOHNSON SNYDER** (Eliza Jane Brown, Nehemiah (Jr)) was born on 12 Jan 1850 in Round Hill, Greenwich, CT. She died on 07 Feb 1940 in Battle Creek, MI. She married James M. Clark, son of Chauncey H. Clark and Mary C. Corwin on 27 Dec 1871 in Greenwich, CT. He was born on 29 Jan 1851 in Middletown, Orange, NY. He died on 06 Aug 1922 in Tulsa, Oklahoma.
Cornelia Johnson Snyder and James M. Clark had the following children:

i.   ADA HAZEL CLARK was born on 16 Apr 1874 in Middletown, NY?. She died on 02 Jan 1941 in Battle

        Creek, MI. She married Joseph Harris, son of Joseph Harris and Lenah Williams on 29 Apr 1909 in Chicago, IL. He was born on 05 Mar 1875 in Wiconisco, Dauphin Co., PA. He died on 25 June 1966 in Battle Creek, MI .

ii.   UNKNOWN TWIN CLARK was born on 16 Apr 1873.

iii.   ELIZABETH LOVERAGE CLARK was born on 07 July 1876 in Brooklyn, New York. She died on 05 Jan 1953 in Detroit, Michigan (Oak Hill cemetery, BC). She married Willis Halem Mitchell, son of William Dwight Mitchell and Margaret A Hallum on 17 Apr 1911 in Downers Grove, IL. He was born in 1882 in Minoa, NY. He died on 24 July 1969 in Detroit, Michigan (Oak Hill cemetery, BC).

16.   **WARD BEECHER SNYDER** (Eliza Jane Brown, Nehemiah (Jr)) was born on 23 Dec 1852 in Round Hill, Greenwich, CT. He died on 29 Oct 1916 in Madison NJ (Christ Church Cemetery, South Amboy, NJ). He married (1) **MARY B. APPLEGATE**, daughter of Charles Applegate and Mary Morse in 1878. She was born on 15 Dec 1857 in South Amboy (Middlesex) NJ. She died on 30 Dec 1944 in Glenridge, (Essex) NJ (Christ Church Cemetery, South Amboy, NJ). He married (2) **WINIFORD CARROLL** on 17 Jan 1874 in Manhattan, NYC. She was born in June 1855. She died in 1915.
        Ward Beecher Snyder and Mary B. Applegate had the following children:

i.   ELIZABETH (BESSIE) SNYDER was born on 02 May 1879 in NJ. She died in 1966 in Lincoln Park, Morris, NJ. She married WILLIAM BALDWIN AXFORD. He was born1872 in NJ. He died on 27 July 1948 in Morristown, Morris, NJ.

ii.   GEORGE L. SNYDER was born in Apr 1880. He died before 1890.

iii.   BEULAH SNYDER was born on 16 Oct 1884 in New York City. She died on 13 Sep 1949 in Fair Haven, Monmouth, NJ. She married (1) AMIEL GUSTAVE ZIMMERMAN on 02 Sep 1900 in Old Bridge, (Middlesex) NJ. He was born on 09 May 1878 in Perth Amboy, NJ. He died on 16 Aug 1927 in Bonnie Burns (TB) Sanitarium, Scotch Plains, (Union) NJ. She married (2) FRANCIS VEERE LAUDER on 20 Oct 1925 in Orange, (Essex) NJ. He was born in 1865. He died on 09 Oct 1930.

iv.   JAMES IRVING SNYDER was born on 22 July 1886 in New Jersey. He died on 20 Feb 1960 in Morristown, NJ (Hackettstown, NJ (Union Cemetery)). He married MABEL CLYMER. She was born on 18 June 1888 in Philadelphia, PA. She died on 11 Jan 1965 in Greensboro, NC.

Ward Beecher Snyder and Winiford Carroll had the following child:

vi.   ARTHUR WARD SNYDER was born in Apr 1881 in New York City. He died on 03 Sep 1908 in Perth Amboy, Middlesex, New Jersey, USA. He married Eleanot Amanda Nosesa Ringquist on 25 June 1906 in Manhattan, NYC.

Chapter 24

Brown Homestead 1906

The following article was published in the New York Times newspaper on May 20, 1906. It is an interview with the last Brown ancestor to live in the old Brown Homestead. It is now called the Brown Kingsworth House and is in the historical district of Round Hill next to the Methodist Church. Only the Salt Box portion (small end) of the house is original. This is the location where Nehemiah Brown Sr. lived, and both Nehemiah Jr. and Major Brown were born. I believe Miss Amy Brown would be a descendant of Major by his daughter Electra as this was the house he occupied in the early 1800s. Nehemiah Jr. lived across the street to the west (no longer standing) as this is the land he willed to his three daughters.

<u>Old Homestead Sold</u>
<u>After 250 Years Tenure</u>

Brown Estate on Old Rye Grant in Winchester
Transferred for the First Time Since 1660

At least 1,000 families, most of whom live in and around New York, are descended from the men who received by grant from King Charles II, in 1660, some 10,00 acres of land on which the town of Rye was the first settlement.

The boundaries of the grant were thus set in the original document: "From Mamaroneck River to Byrum River along the shore, and 12 miles back"

All original papers were destroyed in a fire more than 100 years ago, but the records show that the grant was made to forty-one families, some of which bore the following names, all well known in New York: Brown, Horton, Denham, Purdy, Lane, Frost, Disbrow, Merritt, Hyatt, Hoyt, Knapp, Pease, Kniffin, Odell, Gaipin, Budd, Lounsbury, Travis, Stockham, Fowler, Walter, Cox, Jeffery, Sherwood, Lyon, and Brondig (Brundage).

The grant was made in the name of "Samuel and Deliverance Brown and others." Of Rye, England, in consideration of their loyalty to the King, and it was a royal demesne which they came over here to inhabit.

Through the long period of frontier and colonial life they shared with the rest of the inhabitants of these shores and dangers from Indians and from disease, the rigorous winters, and the rivalries and bickering's which too often threatened their existence and destroyed their peace.

Only one small tract of the vast grant has remained in the original family down to the present time, and this property, consisting of about 100 acres, has just been sold to Aaron A. Carpenter, a wealthy resident of Port Chester.

+   +   +   +   +

The tenacity and ruggedness of the Brown family, which still resides on the old place are evidenced in the person of Miss Amy Brown, a Maiden lady, who was born in 1818, and who, at the age of 93 years, is still active, and decidedly interested in all that is passing about her. I had a pleasant interview with Miss Brown the other day, and her conversation carried one back to a world which has entirely passed away and been eclipsed by the period of modern science and development.

She has an intimate recollection of the world with no railroads, no telegraphs, and indeed, with none of the great comforts of the world of the last fifty years.

In consenting to the sale of an estate which had been in her family for nearly 250 years. One of the oldest records of a white family on this continent. Miss Brown stipulated that she was to have the occupancy of the old homestead so long as she survives.

"There was no reason for us to keep the land any longer," she said, "as there are no direct male heirs to take care of or improve it, and the few surviving women of the family can do better with the proceeds of the sale than holding the property."

Miss Brown has a bright and lively disposition, and is fond of meeting an conversing with strangers. She shows none of the evidence of great age except her failing sight. Her hearing is good; her memory excellent.

Her cousin, Ethan Allen Brown, a son of her father's brother, moved

Front of the Brown house from the gardens.

from the old estate to Ohio early in the last century, went into politics, and served as Governor of Ohio from 1818 to 1822. After he had retired from politics, and was living near Cincinnati, in 1836, Miss Brown visited him at the Western metropolis. Her story of the journey was told with a girl's enthusiasm.

The party went up the Hudson to Albany on a small steamboat with a stern propeller, making the trip in something over two days. From Albany they traveled to Schenectady over a little inland railroad recently built. Thence they journeyed to Buffalo by canal boat, then up Lake Erie to Cleveland by sailing vessel; from Cleveland to a point on the headwaters of the Ohio River by stage, and then down the river by steamboat, which had to wait for a freshet to provide enough water to float the craft.

She remained in the West for two years. When Miss Brown returned to New York, in 1830, she came by stage to Harrisburg, Penn.; then by rail to Baltimore, and the rest of the way by water.

+   +   +   +   +

One of the singularities about this ancient inhabitant of Westchester County and the old Rye grants the fact that she has never had her picture taken and will not consent to having it done. When I sent a photographer to make a view of the old homestead of the Brown's I was in hopes that we might be able to manage a portrait of its interesting occupant. But all of our shrewd projects fell to the ground. She is a tall and stately woman, and it is easy to discern from the regular and classic lines of her face that she must have been a decidedly handsome women in her day. Nothing could induce her to move into a modern house. She is determined to pass her last hour in the home where she was born.

+ +   +   +   +

Situated in one of the most picturesque sections of Westchester County, this old homestead of the Brown family is a really delightful place. The view from a high ridge in the centre of the farm carries the eye over the housetops of Port Chester across the sound to Oyster Bay, and to the sun-lit line of this great Sound where it widened out to the eastward.

On all hands rise the modern villas of rich and cultured people, alternating with the less pretentious homes of Americans who are not millionaires, but who dwell in plenty and peace among their families and friends, doubtless as sane and happy a people as live on the earth today.

How quaint and curious the old place looks amid its modern surroundings! Reminiscences of the old Colonial days are sure to arise in such a place. The ancient "Kings Highway," now called King Street, passed by the door of the old farmhouse, which stands on the very foundation stones that were laid soon after the colonists reached these shores in 1660.

One of the cousins of Miss Amy Brown was Charge d' Affaires of the United States in Brazil under President Jackson and the family has always been prominent in local affairs. Judge Nehemiah Brown, for many years County Judge of Westchester, was also her cousin.

In the Revolution the family activity espoused the American cause, and many important conferences of the leaders were held in the old house. It was a convenient place for the chiefs from south of New York to meet with the New England patriots, as there was ready access by both land and water, and the facilities for "underground" information by this route were well organized. Miss Brown heard her father tell of many interesting events which were not set down in the histories of that period.

In the French and Indian wars, it was also a place of meeting of sturdy defenders of the Anglo-Saxon outposts of the New World. A remnant of a French contingent which had been cut off further up the State tried to escape by the way of Rye and was wiped out by the English on the Brown farms. The last of the hunted Frenchmen took refuge in the cellar of the farmhouse, where he was discovered and shot.

+   +   +   +   +

Even at a period in the memory of Miss Amy Brown a small party of the Poningo tribe of Indians had a camp on the property near where the town of Harrison now stands, and their chief was a frequent friendly visitor to the homestead, Miss Brown and other members of the family also visited the Indian camp, and the young folks often went there to watch the sports of the young redskins.

More than one member of the Brown family served in General Washington's Westchester Guards, and the men of the family were always active in military affairs. The fire previously referred to destroyed most of the ancient belongings of the family, and only a few antiques in the way of furniture and china remain. On the wall of the sitting room hangs a commission dated Sept 10, 1801, signed by George Clinton, Governor, and by Thomas W. Ford, Secretary of the Commonwealth, making Nehemiah Brown a Lieutenant in the Militia.

Many incidents might be recounted to indicate that the old homestead now passing from the control of the very family which redeemed it from the wilderness is, indeed, historic ground, wrapping within its archives an epitome of the country's annals. Already the representatives of some of the families which date their American existence to that spot are making pilgrimages to the ancient homestead on the "King's Highway," where they receive a hearty welcome from Amy Brown, now aged 93 years.   J.A. Mck.

Below is a photo of the west end of the Brown Kingsworth house currently at Round Hill.

Chapter 25

James M. Clark

James M. Clark was born in January 1850 in Middletown, New York. He was the son of Chauncey H. Clark and Mary C. Corwin. The obituary of his father Chauncy referred to James as J. Mortimer Clark. There is no other reference to his complete middle name. Chauncy's first wife was Angeline Slauson, and she bore three children, Albert H., Nancy, and Emeline. These half-siblings were 14, 12, and 10 years older than James. After the death of Angeline, Chauncey remarried Mary Corwin and bore James followed by his sister Alice ten years later.

On December 27, 1871, James married Cornelia Snyder in her hometown of Greenwich, Connecticut. They initially lived in Middletown, NY where they had their first children. Their second daughter was born in Brooklyn, New York on July 7, 1875.

James was employed as a salesman for Peck & Snyder Sporting Goods in New York City. Peck and Snyder were started by Andrew Peck and Irving Snyder (brother of Cornelia) and were located at 124-128 Nassau Street. The company was noted for its invention of the first rubber-soled and canvas tennis shoe, the first baseball cards, and the peck & Snyder baseballs including the "dead ball", ice skates, and flat-top tennis rackets. It is believed that Cornelia worked at Peck & Snyder before the birth of their children.

In 1875 James became embroiled in a Snyder family conflict which resulted in him spending a short time in jail. Cornelia's mother (Eliza Brown Snyder) moved from Greenwich to New York City with her younger children, because of her divorce from Cornelia's father, William Snyder. It appears that James and his brother-in-law, Ward Snyder, devised a plan to get Eliza's furniture and other personal belongings out of the Snyder homestead in Round Hill, Greenwich back to New York City. James took the lead role in this operation. Reportedly, James arrived early in the morning and William woke to find him seated at the kitchen table. James, as well as the Snyder siblings, had other encounters with William and were not allowed to be in the Round Hill house. James stated he had a gun, had two wagons, and hired help to load up the furniture and other personal belongings. They packed up kitchen furnishings, beds, linens, a piano, pictures, furniture, etc. They got to Port Chester, New York, and loaded the goods on a rail car. William followed closely and obtained a warrant for James's arrest for grand larceny. Ward Snyder came to his rescue and a settlement was made by paying 25% of the value of the furniture to William.

According to census information, James and his family lived in Philadelphia for a few years around 1880. By 1883 James, Cornelia, and the two girls were living in Chicago. In 1885 James created a baitcasting fishing rod made of 6 ft. split bamboo with a straight grip and a reel seat above the handle. It was marketed by John Wilkinson Co. of Chicago in 1890, which was his employer. This short rod was unique and became very popular for casting baits for bass in rivers and shorelines where trees limited your casting. Newspaper articles in the 1890s would cover the fishing scene where many affluent anglers gained notoriety. There were tales of James M. Clark (or J.M. Clark) on excursions to lakes and streams in northern Wisconsin with bounties of 25-65 bass in one day weighing 2 to 5 pounds each. Articles detailed trips within 90 miles of Chicago as well, where he would fish for black bass, smallmouth bass, walleye, and muskie. An article in 1896 referred to James M. Clark, a veteran angler, who frequently fished Cedar Lake 38 miles south of Chicago and never failed to land less than twenty-five black bass a day. In September of 1897, the newspaper chronicled articles on a twelve-day fishing tour that took him to the Turtle Lake system (northern Wisconsin). The article stated, "Mr. Clark was widely acquainted with that part of the country and had a superior knowledge of angling". He gained the nickname "Uncle James". He also made trips to Northern Lower Michigan where he would fish the Au Sable River for trophy trout.

At the 1893 World's Columbian Exposition (World's Fair) James competed in a Baitcasting tournament in which he placed 2nd, averaging over 103 feet per cast. The Wilkinson Co. sold Clark's bait casting rod, Clark's Combination rod, Clark's trolling rod, and other Clark rods. This rod was manufactured for James by Fred D. Divine Co, of Utica NY. They were made initially, from Lancewood, not Bamboo.

Sometime around 1900 James left Cornelia and the now adult daughters (now 25 and 27 yrs. old) and moved to Kansas City, Missouri. He became employed as a salesman at Schmelzer Arms Sporting Goods. At Schmelzer Arms, he managed the fishing department and was nicknamed "Dad" as he was over 50 years old at that time. On a float trip, down the Current River in central Missouri. Clark, with his companions, caught 350 Black Bass in six days. In 1908 James was listed by the "National Association of Scientific Angling Club" as a member of the "Roll of Honor", and ineligible to compete for special prizes. One magazine article said "Dad" or J. M. Clark as he is rightly named is found at the main street store of the Schmelzer Arms Co. He is a courteous, White-haired gentleman of the old school, whose ruddy cheeks tell of the days spent in the open. Mr. Clark is said to breathe, dream and eat fish. He could tell you of days spent with the late Chief Justice Fuller, whom he taught how to cast a fly, and with Ex-President Harrison, who had to come to Mr. Clarks' way of reeling. The article goes on to tell of Clark's fly fishing in the Rocky Mountains.

James would occasionally write to Cornelia as she had moved to Michigan, but Cornelia never responded. In census and city directories James listed himself as married, but Cornelia shows up as widowed. Any photos of James were absent from the family. Even though James listed himself as married (living alone) in the 1920 census, he would remarry Ida, in 1921, and move to Tulsa, Oklahoma. His obituary in The Tulsa Daily World from August 7, 1922, reads as follows.

J.M. Clark, 71, passed away at his home at 116 W. Cameron Street, Sunday (6th) morning at 8 o'clock. He is survived by his widow. He was born in Middletown, N.Y. in 1851. He moved west in the early days and for 23 years was connected with the Smeltzer Arms store in Kansas City. He was the originator of the bait casting rod while employed there. He came to Tulsa about a year ago. Funeral services will be held at the residence Monday afternoon at 4 o'clock.

George and Robert Harris, his grandsons, were told that James was disappointed because he never had a son. Sadly, George & Robert never met their grandfather. James Clark is buried alone, in Rose Hill Memorial Park in Tulsa.

At the time of his death, Cornelia, Florence, Ada & Joseph and the two boys, George and Robert were staying at a cottage on Fine Lake, just north of Battle Creek, MI. A telegram was sent to Cornelia informing her of his death, but the boys remember very little being said about this.

Chapter 26

Chauncey Clark & Mary Corwin

Chauncy Clark (1814-1883) & Mary C. Corwin (1825-1890) (2nd Great Grandparents)
James Mortimer Clark
Ada Hazel Clark
George Clark Harris
David Joseph Harris

Chauncey was born in 1814 in Orange County, New York, south west of the town of Middletown. He was the oldest of seven born to Hulet Clark and Mary (Hallock) Clark. They lived on a farm near the town of Greenville, NY.

When Chauncey was 11 years old, a dysentery outbreak took the lives of his mother Mary (September 2, 1825) and five of his six younger siblings (August 1825)- all within a 16-day period. Dysentery is an infectious disease that causes inflammation of the intestines resulting in severe diarrhea with blood. Dysentery infection is transmitted through fecal oral route indirectly through contaminated water and food. In the 1800's treatment for dysentery consisted of a mixture of leaves from a pine tree with water and egg white. Today it would be treated with antibiotics. They are all buried in the Manning Cemetery in Greenville, Orange County, NY. Chauncy's uncle and grandfather (Zebulon Hallock) also died shortly after his mother, also of dysentery. It is said they are buried in the same grave in the Hallock/Blizzard cemetery about two miles from the Manning cemetery.

One year after Chauncey lost his family, his father, Hulet, remarried (Emeline Forbes). When he was 14, his father purchased a 420-acre farm just north of Westtown (Orange County) on S. Plank Road. I assume Chauncey started his lifelong farm work here. This new farm was only about 5 miles east from Greenville. Chauncey would have six half siblings from his father's second marriage. Many of these half siblings were well-connected in the Orange County area. The land owned by Hulet has been passed down to later generations of Chauncy's half siblings.

Chauncey (age 20) married his first wife, Angeline Slauson in 1835. From that marriage, he had three children, Albert, Emeline and Nancy. In 1845 (age 30) he married his second wife, Mary C. Corwin (1825-1890). She was 20. Mary would be my second great grandmother. From that union he had two children, James Mortimer (my great grandfather) and Alice. So, James Clark (my great Grandfather) had three step-siblings between 9 and 13 years older. His full sister was ten years younger.

Chauncey farmed in Wallkill, which is about five miles east by northeast of Middletown. In 1845, he farmed 111 acres with $50 worth of machinery, one horse and two working oxen. He had 23 milch cows and four other cattle. He produced 200 bushel of Indian corn, 30 bushel of potatoes, 50 bushel of buckwheat and 60 tons of hay. In 1880, when he was 65, he rented his farmland. From 68 acres he produced 6,000 gallons of milk and 3,120 dozen eggs, as well as other crops. In 1880, he was in Wawayanda, which is five miles south by southwest of Middletown or about halfway between the original Clark land and Middletown. Chauncy had to be a hard worker because in 1845, his children were not old enough to help farming. Can you imagine one person milking 23 cows twice a day, by hand, and farming with no motorized equipment. Here is some trivia I recently learned. How was the amount of land in one acre determined? It is about 209 feet by 209 feet square. An acre is the amount of land that can be plowed by a team of oxen in one day.

In 1869, Chauncey and his wife Mary joined the Congregational Church in Middletown where she had attended since a child. Chauncey died on Feb 1, 1883 and is buried in Hillside cemetery in a plot with his daughter (by first marriage) Emeline Ogden's family. Emeline was just 9 years old when her mother died, and she was very close to her step-mother Mary Corwin Clark.

Little is known of Mary Corwin. She lived at 38 south street, in Middletown, after Chauncey's death. When she died in 1890, she was living at her son-in-law's house at 3 Spring Street. The obituary states: She was married to Chauncey H. Clark and three children were the result of a happy union. Two of them survive, James M. Clark, now of Chicago, and Alice R., wife of Mr. Chas. H. Emde, of this city. A stepdaughter is the wife of Mr. Geo. T. Ogden of this city, and Oliver B. Corwin, Waverly, N.Y., and Mrs. Adeline Doyle, wife of Mr. Wm. Doyle, of Howells, are relatives of the deceased. Mary is buried next to Chauncey in the Hillside cemetery in Middletown. They are in the plot owned by George Ogden.

When Mary married Chauncy, she was 22 years old and had an instant family with three children- one boy and two girls aged 8, 6 and 4. Emeline, being the youngest, was close to her new mother and even after Chauncy's death Emeline looked after her stepmother. In Mary's obituary it was written, "Mrs. Clark was one whom to know was to love a good, true woman in every sense of the word. She had been a member of the Congregational Church here ever since her childhood. Her death will cause sorrow among a large circle of friends and relatives".

Mary Corwin's ancestors are William, Eli, David, David, John, John, Matthias all on the direct Corwin line. Matthias was the first Corwin to come to America and settled on Long Island. David Corwin, father of Eli, moved from Long Island to Orange County, NY. David was one of the founding members of the Middletown Congregational church in 1785. The church was established about 100 years before the town of Middletown.

Chapter 27

Hulet H. Clark
(3GGF)

Judge Hulet Clark was born in Bedford, Westchester Co., N. Y., March 26, 1790. His childhood was spent at home, and the common schools were his only educational advantages. In 1812, he married Mary, daughter of Zebulon Hallock, of Greenville, and their children were Chauncey H., who married Angeline Slauson, and afterwards Mary Corwin, and lives in Wawayanda; Alfred, Bertha, Samuel J., James Monroe, Henry Hallock, and Zebulon H., all of whom died in August 1826. His wife Mary died Sept. 2, 1825.

Hulet's father, Caleb Clark moved to Otisville, Orange Co., N. Y., about 1796, and a few years afterwards into Minisink township, where he died in 1840. His grandfather David was of English descent, and lived and died in Westchester Co., N. Y. Caleb, father of Judge Hulet Clark, was born in Westchester County in 1760. David, married Jemima Kniffen, and their children were Hulet, of whom this sketch is written; Wallace, married Sarah Smith; Jerusha, married Moses Durland, and lives in Greenville; David, married Nancy Slauson, and after her death Betsy Manning; Phebe, married Lewis Seybolt; Jas. F., married Abbie Hallock, and lives in Greenville

Hulet married Mary Hallock in 1812. He was 22 and she was 19 years old. They lived within two miles of each other. Soon after his marriage, Judge Clark commenced farming on the farm now owned by Hulet Manning, of Greenville. That farm is very close to the Manning Cemetery and other lands owned by Hulet's brothers.

After 14 years of marriage and the births of seven children, a dysentery outbreak devastated the family in August of 1826. Mary and five of her seven children died within a 16-day period. Mary died on September 2nd. They are buried in the Manning cemetery near that original farm. Hulet was left with two surviving children, Chauncey, the oldest, was 10, and Zebulon H. was just 2 years old. Hulet remarried just two months after the death of Mary. I imagine Hulet would have too many painful memories to stay on that farm as he sold it to Hulet Manning and bought another farm a few miles south. Nov. 30, 1826, Judge Clark married (2nd marriage) Emeline, widow of John Greenleaf and daughter of Ephraim and Amy Forbes, of New London, Conn. Of this union were born Bertha, who lives on the old homestead; William H., who married Emily, daughter of Robert Robertson, of Wawayanda, and lives in Minisink; Caleb, who married Phebe A., daughter of Henry Decker of Minisink; Elizabeth C, who married Gilbert W. Roe, and lives in Oshkosh, Wis.; and George Dallas, who lives on the old homestead. Emeline Clark died June 2, 1876.

On April 1, 1828, Hulet purchased his new farm. Local records indicate the house was built around 1800 by a farmer named Wadsworth to serve a parcel that at the time included 420 acres. Clark, who had come from Westchester County with his family around the same time at the age of six, served as an officer in the state militia and as town clerk during the early 1820s. He bought the Wadsworth farm in 1828 after the death of his first wife and several children during a dysentery outbreak, while he was also serving as town justice. He lived there for the rest of his life, eventually becoming town supervisor and chairing the county's Board of Supervisors a few years before his death in 1857. Local lore holds that the house was a station on the Underground Railroad, but no evidence has yet been found to verify this.

In 1814, he received a commission as captain of a company in the One Hundred and Forty-eighth New York Regiment of militia from Governor Tompkins, which he held for six years. He was afterwards commissioned major, and served until 1826, when he was again commissioned as colonel of the same regiment by Governor DeWitt Clinton and served for eight consecutive years. He was town clerk in 1819-20, justice of the peace from 1821 to 1834 and judge of the Court of Common Pleas from 1834 to 1840.

The **Hulet Clark Farmstead** is located along South Plank Road north of the hamlet of Westtown, in the Town of Minisink, New York. It is a 75-acre property along both sides of the road, consisting of a farmhouse, barn, chicken coop and other outbuildings. While he did not build the house, Clark, a longtime Minisink resident who served the town in several different capacities in the first half of the 19th century, would be most associated with it

The center of the Clark farm is the farmhouse, a two-story hand-hewn three-bay timber frame structure. Its stone foundation is built into the sloping ground beneath, with four feet of exposure in front. A porch was built in the 1930s to replace a more modest stoop that preceded it, along with the house's stone chimney, and a small south addition replaced a larger one earlier in the 20th century. The interior floor plan remains largely unaltered

In 1876, his heirs began subdividing the land. The current property remained a profitable family-owned dairy farm into the 1920s. After a few other changes of ownership, it became property of the Pine family in 1933, who began the poultry operations that continued until they divested themselves of the farm in 1950. The new owners, the Hulles, continued to raise chickens for a few more years but have leased the fields to neighboring farmers since the 1960s. The farm was added to the National Register of Historic Places in 1998 due to both Clark's importance in town history and the farmhouse's status as a mostly intact sample of the rural vernacular architecture practiced by Americans of British descent in the early years of the United States.

Politically he was a Democrat, represented his town in the board of supervisors, and was chairman of that body in 1851. Judge Clark was an active, energetic businessman. He kept his engagements with scrupulous integrity and was regarded as a man of sterling worth and a representative man of his time. He was a director of the Highland Bank of Newburgh for many years. He was a man of positive character, and although dignified in his bearing, was Democratic in his principles to a large degree. He died March 31, 1857.

Chapter 28

Mary Hallock Clark - A Life Remembered

In this chapter, we delve into the remarkable biography of Mary Hallock, my third great-grandmother, whose legacy continued through her son Chauncy, grandson James M. Clark, followed by Ada Clark Harris, then George Clark Harris.

Early Life and Family

Mary Hallock was born on October 15, 1792, in Orange County, New York, a place steeped in history. Her parents, Zebulon Hallock III and Bethiah Booth, had migrated to Minisink, Orange County, from Suffolk County on Long Island. This migration was part of a broader movement of Long Island residents to Orange County, both before, during, and after the Revolutionary War.

Mary's life began in Minisink, and she grew up alongside her younger two brothers & three sisters. Many cousins on her father's side lived in the same vicinity. Her family, like many in the area, were hard working farmers, cultivating the land to sustain their lives.

Marriage and Family Life

At the young age of 20, Mary married Hulet Clark, a man two years her senior. Over the course of their 13-year marriage, they welcomed seven children into their lives. In the absence of slaves, children played an integral role in the farm's operations. White farmers who did not own slaves were called Yeoman.

The Clark family's farm was situated approximately two miles north of the village of Greenville, within the town (township) of Minisink, Orange County. Their farm shared its borders with the farms of Hulet's brother, Wallace, and his father, Caleb, creating a tight-knit agricultural community.

During these years, Hulet Clark wore many hats. He worked as a farmer, served as a town supervisor, and even served in the New York Military. Life in rural Orange County was demanding, but Mary and Hulet persevered, raising their children with love and care.

The Tragedy

Tragedy struck the Clark family in August 1825. Samuel, their 7-year-old son, succumbed to dysentery, a devastating disease prevalent in colonial times. Dysentery, also known as "Camp fever" or "the Bloody flux," was caused by bacterial infections. Mary's family, like many others, faced the risks associated with this illness, transmitted through contaminated food and water.

Samuel's death marked the beginning of a heart-wrenching ordeal. Within eight days, four more of Mary and Hulet's children fell ill to dysentery and passed away. James, aged 3, followed Samuel, and then Bertha, aged 9, and Alfred, aged 10, passed away in quick succession. Henry, aged 5, became the fifth child to succumb to the disease.

Five of their seven children were lost within a span of just eight days. The pain and grief must have been unimaginable.

Legacy and Resting Place

Mary herself passed away just eight days after her fifth child's death, on September 3, 1825. She rests alongside her children in the Manning cemetery, her headstone marking the end of an era.

In the early 1800s, it was common for families to bury their loved ones on their farms, a practice that must have made dealing with loss even more difficult. The Manning cemetery, located on a corner of their farm, had only thirteen burials before the devastating loss of these five young lives.

Aftermath and New Beginnings

Following Mary's death, Hulet made the difficult decision to sell the farm attached to the Manning cemetery. He acquired a larger 420-acre farm about three miles south in the heart of Minisink Valley, seeking more fertile land. Hulet remarried and started a new family in his new home. Mary's youngest child, Zebulon H. Clark, was about one year old when Mary passed. He passed away at the age of 18 and was buried next to his mother and siblings in the Manning cemetery. Chauncy, who was 9 years old at the time of his mother's death, lived to the age of 67, continuing the family's farming tradition in the Minisink area of Orange County.

The story of Mary Hallock Clark is intertwined with the history of Minisink, a town that witnessed both the joys and sorrows of her life. Today, Minisink remains a township in Orange County, a place where Mary's legacy endures through the generations. History books of Orange County tell of her story.

The rest of the story as Paul Harvey used to say

Many times, today when someone dies or as another life event occurs, we often say, it's time to update our will. Zebulon Hallock, Mary's father, seeing how short life can be, decided to write his will while he still could. Just two weeks after Mary's death, Zebulon got it done. He had two boys and five girls, one now deceased. In the 1600-1900 period most large family wills would leave half or more of all land to the oldest son with the rest of the land divided between the other boys. The girls might get a small amount of money and something from the farm, like china, beds, quilts, a saddle, or sometimes an animal. Zebulon's will gave all his land to be divided equally between his two boys Zebulon (Jr) and Daniel B. He also made provision for his wife Bethiah to keep two good milch cows and a bedroom in their home. Zebulon then gave each of the living girls money ($50), that would be Ruth (27), Bethiah (25), Elizabeth (23) and Hannah (29). For Mary (32) he left $75 each to her surviving Two children, Chauncy (9) and Zebulon (1), their last names being Clark not given in the will. The will was not to be executed for ten years or the death of his wife Bethiah.

Timeline fall of 1825 Minisink, Orange Co. NY.:

Aug 17 – 24 Five children die from dysentery. We could say nine uneventful days but Mary and possibly others were at the edge of death.
Sept 2 Mary Hallock Clark, deceased

The rest of the story:

Sept 7 Mary's cousin Luther whose farm is next to her father's farm, loses two children aged 2 & 7 to dysentery.
Sept 10 Mary's cousin loses another child at age 9.
Sept 16 Mary's father Zebulon makes a will as his nephew is losing more children to dysentery.
Sept 17 Mary's cousin loses two more children aged 1 and 5. Only their oldest of 6 children would survive.
Oct 4 Zebulon loses his 22-year-old son, Zebulon to dysentery. This is Mary's brother, and he lived with his father. He was to receive half of the land after his father's death.
Oct 5 Zebulon Hallock, Mary's father, is taken by dysentery.
Both Mary's father Zebulon and brother Zebulon are the first recorded burials on a high hill of the Zebulon Hallock farm. It was said they were buried together. The will would now leave all the land to Daniel.

The Clark's (Caleb) settled in the area just north of the Manning cemetery. On today's map from I-84 and Mountain Road go northeast on Mountain Road about one mile, it will be on the left. The Hallock's had four families settled in Minisink Israel, Zebulon, William H., and Joseph. They and their offspring owned land at the corner of Fort Van Tyle Road and Mullock Road. This is about two miles northeast of the Manning cemetery. They owned land on all four corners of this intersection at one time or another. The private cemetery where the Hallock's are buried is 0.2 miles southeast of that corner and about 100 yards to the right side up a hill and in the woods, not visible from the road and completely overgrown.

Chapter 29

Origins of Clarks in America

Samuel Clark (8th GGF) is believed to be our Clark's earliest documented ancestor. From "Huntington's History of Stamford" and the records, we learn: Samuel Clark came to Wethersfield in 1636. Having become dissatisfied with the Westfield Colony, he was "one of the companies of restless and dissatisfied men" who forsook the colony and was one of twenty men who bound themselves on May 16th, 1640, to establish for themselves a home at Rippowam, now called Stamford, CT. Samuel is listed on each of the first three lists made of the Stamford settlement. On the first assignment of lands, he was allotted 7 acres. Samuel Clark b. about 1619. He married Hannah Fordham. They had a large and dispersed family. They were in Milford, Connecticut by 1669; to Hempstead, Long Island County, New York; and, in 1685, to New Haven, Connecticut, where it is thought that he died, about 1690. He was living with his son Samuel Jr. at the time of his death.

William Clark Sr. (7th GGF) was born at Stanford in 1645. He had three boys we know of: William Jr (6th GGF) b.1662, Nathan b. 1666, and Joseph. In 1680, William with fifteen others purchased on the 23rd of December, the land where the town of Bedford (Hop Lands) now stands, from chiefs of Mohegan Indians. In 1690, ten years later, William Sr. was 45, and William Jr was 28 years old. They (with Nathan 24) moved from Stamford by way of Pound Ridge, 13 miles north. There were 31 inhabitants in the township at that time. The last land purchase from the Mohegans was in 1703. In 1704, Bedford encompassed 23,000 acres to its 29 landholders, three of whom were William Sr, William Jr, and Nathan Clarke. William Sr. died in 1712 in Bedford. William Clark married Susanna Trott (Treat) in Stamford on 17 August 1668. Susanna was born in about 1650.

One record shows that Nathan Clark lived and died on the east side of the street, halfway up the hill, nearly opposite the 2nd Presbyterian church, ¼ mile north of the village of Bedford, where his father William Sr. also lived and died.

William Clark Jr (6th GGF) was born in 1662. He and his Father were two among 16 men who purchased land from the Indians on 23 Dec 1680 and established the township of Bedford, NY. He married Hannah and had John (abt. 1695), William, Ebenezer, David, and Joseph. As a side note, this John (1695) brother of our David (1708) was a hatter by trade, though hunting and trapping was his favorite amusement. His constitution and faculties continued to a great age, so much so that he made a hat after he was 100 years old. He died in the time of the

Revolutionary War. He dwindled to a mere skeleton. His daughter Hannah took care of him. I have the story from her mouth that she could handle him as she could a baby; and when the British Light Horse burned the town of Bedford [11 July 1779], they, after plundering the house in which he lay, were about to set fire to it, when his nursing daughter on her knees with uplifted hands prayed them to desist on account of her aged parent that was unable to be moved. The ravages of a destroying army were for once turned aside and the old man was allowed to die a natural death." (by this John would have only been 84 at the time of the burning?) While Both William Sr & Jr. Clark died in Bedford there are no cemetery records or headstones from that time (before 1750).

David Clark (5th GGF) was born in 1708 in Bedford, Westchester, NY. He was married twice and had children with both wives. From his first wife Abigail Smith, they had David, Jacob, William, Keziah, and Sarah. From his second wife Sarah Dann (a widow) he had Hannah, Caleb, Samuel, Silas, and Nehemiah. On July 11, 1779, the British burned all the buildings in Bedford destroying any old homesteads. David died about 1773, in Westchester, New York Colony, British Colonial America, at the age of 65. A Clark record from 1852 indicates that he moved to Orange Co. and then on to Ontario and died there. Sarah died at age 96 in 1823 in Ulster County, NY.

Caleb Clark (4th GGF) was born in 1760 in Bedford. Caleb's father would have been 52 when he was born. Caleb Clark moved to Otisville, Orange Co., N. Y., about 1796, and a few years afterward into Minisink township, where he died in 1840. He is buried in the Manning cemetery near Greenville, with his wife Jemima Kniffen.

Hulet H. Clark (3rd GGF) (Caleb's son) was born in 1790 in Bedford and moved as a child to Minisink, Orange Co. NY, There are accounts of Judge Hulet Clark in the book, "History of Orange county". Hulet's son Chauncy, Grandson James, and Great Granddaughter Ada Hazel Clark (my grandmother) were all born in Orange Co.

Samuel Clark b. Abt 1619, Devonshire, England, d. 1690, New Haven, CT
Hannah Fordham b. 1622, d. 1708
> (other children, Samuel Jr. Joseph, Daniel)

> William Clark Sr. b. 1645, Stamford, CT, d. 1712, Bedford, NY, m. 1668, Stamford
> Susanna Treat b. abt. 1650
> (other children, John, William, Ebenezer, Joseph)

>> William Clark Jr. b. 1662 d. 2 Mar 1728, Bedford, NY
>> Hannah Ayres b. 1673, d. 1710

>>> David Clark b. 1708, Bedford, NY, d. 1773, Bedford, NY
>>> Abigail Smith b. d bef. 1768 (Mother of David) m. 1725
>>> Sarah Dann m. abt 1768 b. 1827, d. 1823 (mother of Caleb)

>>> David Clark b. abt. 1735 **IS NOT A DIRECT ANCESTOR**
>>> Wife: Abigail Sherwood, (1728 -1782)

>>>> Caleb Clark b. 1760, Bedford, NY d. 1740 Minisink, NY
>>>> Jemima Kniffen b. 1762, Bedford, NY d. 1741 Minisink, NY

>>>>> Hulet H. Clark b. 1790 Bedford,
>>>>> d. 1857 Minisink
>>>>> Mary E. Hallock b. 1792, Orange co, NY, d. 1825 Minisink

Conflicts:
Many accounts show Caleb as the son of David Clark b. 1735. Caleb was the son of the first David Clark b. 1708 by his second wife Sarah. This means David was 52 at the birth of Caleb.

Chapter 30

Clark Genealogy
continued from Chauncy & Mary Clark (Middletown, NY)

This chapter will look at the ancestors for Chauncy Clark and Mary Corwin, my second great grandparents. While they both were born and died in Orange County, NY. Their parents and grandparents were also from Orange County. Their great grandparents (right column below) were from other parts of New England.

Chauncey H. Clark
1816 - 1883
b: 1816 in Orange Co, NY
d: 01 Feb 1883 in
Wawayanda, Orange Co.
NY (Hillside Cem.
Middletown)

Hulet H Clark
1790 - 1857
b: 26 Mar 1790 in Bedford,
Westchester, New York,
United States
d: 31 Mar 1857 in Minisink,
Orange Co., NY;
Unionville, Orange County,
New York, USA

Caleb Clark
1760 - 1840
b: 10 Oct 1760 in Bedford,
Westchester Co., NY
d: 30 Apr 1840 in Minisink,
Orange Co., NY; Manning
cemetery. Greenville, NY

David Clark
1708 - 1773
b: 1708 in Bedford,
Westchester Co. NY
d: 1773

William Clark
1670 - 1726

Hannah Ayres
1673 - 1710

Sarah Dann
1727 - 1823
b: 1727
d: 15 Dec 1823 in Ulster,
Ulster, New York, USA

Jemima Kniffen
1762 - 1841
b: 27 Feb 1762 in Bedford,
Westchester Co. NY
d: 09 Dec 1841 in Minisink,
Orange Co., NY; Manning
cemetery. Greenville, NY

Roger Kniffen
1726 - 1798
b: 1726 in Rye,
Westchester, NY
d: 21 Dec 1798 in Rye,
Westchester, NY

Benjamin Kniffen

Gertrude Purdy

Johanna Sniffen
1735 - 1767
b: 1735 in
Rye,Westchester,NY
d: 1767

Mary Patricia Hallock
1792 - 1825
b: 15 Oct 1792 in of,
Orange County, New York
d: 02 Sep 1825 in Orange
Co., NY; Manning
cemetery. Greenville, NY

Zebulon Hallock 3rd
1767 - 1825
b: 28 Jun 1767 in
Mattituck, Suffolk County,
New York
d: 05 Oct 1825 in Hallock &
Blizzard family cemetery

Zebulon Hallock 2nd
1727 - 1814
b: 1727 in Southold, Suffol...
d: 1814 in Minisink, Orang...

Zebulon Hallock Sr.

Martha Reeves

Elizabeth Wells
1745 -
b: 1745 in Cutchogue, Suff...
d: Minisink, Orange, New...

Henry Wells
1714 - 1792

Abigail Dickerson

Bethia Booth
1765 - 1825
b: 13 Oct 1765 in Southold,
Suffolk, NY
d: Aft. 1825

Daniel Booth
1730 - 1812
b: 1730 in
Southold,Suffolk,Ny
d: 07 Jul 1812 in Southold,
Suffolk, New York, United
States

Daniel Booth Sr

Rose Holloway

Ruth Terry
- 1807
d: 11 Apr 1807 in Southold,
Suffold, Long Island, NY

Samuel Terry
1693 - 1762

Naomi Dickerson

127

Notes: Orange county includes the area around Middletown, NY., and includes many small towns like Minisink, Greenville, Wallkill, Wawayanda, and Goshen. Middletown is the biggest town in the area, but it was the last town to be established. It was in the Middle of three towns, Goshen and two others, hence it was called Middletown.

Most references to Suffolk Co. NY are for the towns of Southold, Cutchogue & Mattituck in Suffolk Co. located in the East end of Long Island, only about 4 miles apart.

Southampton, NY is also in Suffolk Co. It was established the same year of 1640 and some of our ancestors came from Southampton as well.

Mary C. Corwin
Mary C. Corwin
1823 - 1890
b: 11 Sep 1823 in Wallkill, Ulster, New York, United States
d: 13 May 1890 in Middletown, NY (2 spring st.)

William W. Corwin
William W. Corwin
1799 - 1837
b: 16 Jul 1799 in Goshen, Orange, N.Y.
d: 1837 in Hillside Cemetery, Middletown, Orange, New York, United States

Eli Corwin
Eli Corwin
1765 - 1826
b: 27 Jan 1765
d: 01 Jun 1826 in Goshen, Orange, New York, United States

David Corwin
David Corwin
1730 - 1794
b: Mar 1730 in Southold, Suffolk, NY
d: 1794 in Middletown, Orange, New York, USA; No headstone found

- **David Corwin** 1708 - 1782
- **Deborah Wells** 1712 - 1798

Abigail Davis
Abigail Davis
1748 - 1794
b: 1748
d: 1794

Mary Wickham
Mary Wickham
1764 - 1842
b: 31 Jul 1764 in Long Island, New York
d: 12 Aug 1842 in Orange Co, NY

Samuel Wickham
Samuel Wickham
1723 - 1778
b: 15 Aug 1723 in Long Isl...
d: 24 Nov 1778

- **Joseph Wickham**
- **Sarah Dymond**

Abigail Howell
Abigail Howell
1719 - 1785
b: 1719
d: 1785

- **Isreal Howell** 1686 - 1739
- **Abigail Cooper**

Matilda Sweezy
Matilda Sweezy
1796 - 1859
b: 1796 in Goshen, Orange, N.Y.
d: 24 Aug 1859 in Middletown, Orange, New York, United States; Hillside Cemetery, Middletown NY

David Sweezey
David Sweezey
1761 - 1832
b: 1761 in Brookhaven,Suffolk,Ny
d: 1832

Chistopher Swezey
Chistopher Swezey
1718 - 1770
b: 1718 in Southold, Suffol...
d: 1770 in Swezeytown, S...

- **Stephen B Swezey**
- **Elizabeth Youngs**

Juliana Davis
Juliana Davis
1731 - 1825
b: 1731 in Southold, Suffolk, New York, USA
d: 20 Oct 1825

Berthia Benjamin
Berthia Benjamin
1760 - 1805
b: 1760
d: 1805

Nathan Benjamin
Nathan Benjamin
1733 - 1805
b: 1733 in Southold, Suffol...
d: 14 May 1805 in Baiting...

- **Nathan Benjamin**
- **Deborah Clark** 1706 - 1736

Jemima Aldrich
Jemima Aldrich
1735 - 1810
b: 1735 in Mattituck, Suffol...
d: 11 Jan 1810 in Baiting H...

- **Jacob Aldrich**

Bedford, NY is in Westchester Co. and is just north of Round Hill, Greenwich CT. David Clark migrated from Bedford, Orange Co. NY by crossing the Hudson River near the location that a chain was placed across the Hudson to prevent the British from advancing their ships further north. There are errors in many of the genealogies concerning David and his wives. He had only one.

The majority of this lineage takes us to Southold, Long Island. Other names going further back on this tree in Southold include last names of: Booth, Horton, Holloway, Terry, Dickenson, Mapes *, Puffier, Paine, Hallock, Reeve, Brown, Purrier and Knight. The cemeteries of Suffolk County are filled with these names. Most are related in some way.

From Mary Corwin, wife of Chauncy we still go back to Suffolk, NY. Those additional surnames include Corwin, Foy, Wells, Youngs, Tuthill, King, Frost and Burton. All of the above right-hand column lived in Suffolk Co., NY.

Do we have any royalty through the Clark line? Yes, Ruth Terry * above had a great grandfather, Thomas Mapes b. 1628 in England, d. 1687 in Southold, NY. Thomas's 12th Great Grandfather was Edward the I, King of England. Back five more generations would be Henry the 1st King of England who was the son of William the Conqueror, King of England. Henry the 1st was his fourth son, and William Kenneth Harris would be his 28th Great Grandson of William the Conqueror.

What is the Southold connection? By going back to the founding of Southold, we might find ancestries leading down to our family lines. That will be covered in the next chapter.

Background: Plymouth Colony, America's first permanent Puritan settlement, was established by English Separatist Puritans in December 1620. The Town of Southold is the first English settlement in the state of New York. It was founded in the year 1640 by a group of thirteen families from the New Haven (Connecticut) Colony. Reverend John Youngs & family were accompanied by 13 other families. Youngs' brother-in-law was Peter Hallock. Barnabas Horton was a baker. William Wells was a lawyer for the group. Thomas Mapes was their surveyor. Others included John Budd, John Conklin, John Swazey, William and John Tuthill. All came with their families except Peter Hallock who later went back for his wife. They doubtless had been on the island prior to this time to check out home sights. The group came from New Haven, CT where they prepared for their settlement. All had been members of Puritan churches and came from Norwalk and Suffolk counties of

England. The settlers landed as a group on October 23, 1640. On nearing the shore, they cast lots to decide who should first set foot on the land. The lot fell on Peter Hallock, and the place where he first stepped upon the land has ever since been known as Hallock's Landing. On coming ashore, they all knelt down and engaged in prayer, Peter Hallock leading, as had been determined by the lot. I have underlined our direct ancestors above. We also have other ancestors who arrived shortly after the first group or were born shortly after arriving. Matthias Corwin is sometimes listed as one of the 13 families. Notice there are only eight families listed above. This story is what has been passed down for many generations and details vary with each telling. Birth dates don't always fall where they should logically to make the landing happen with the people listed. Rev. Youngs was brother-in-law to Peter Hallock, but I don't think our ancestry was through Rev. Youngs sister. Thomas Mapes the surveyor, would only be 12 years old in 1840 and makes it highly unlikely he was married. Hallock's Landing, named after Peter (our 9th Great Grandfather) is now called "Founders Landing" and it is on the south side of the island. That would mean they would sail around the east end of Long Island and land just over ½ mile from Southold Church. There are streets still named for Wells, Hallock and Youngs in the Southold area.

The settlers of Southold brought in the famous Indian fighter, John Underhill, to live in the center of the community at Feather Hill. Fortunately, the Corchaugs were few in number, peace-loving and helpful, so Underhill's services were not needed for long. There was very little crime, and the Indians were less aggressive than in other parts of the country. Long Island was quite isolated from the rest of New England. It was 135 years (four generations) from the founding of Southold to the start of the Revolutionary war. Families stayed on Long Island because it was a comfortable place to live. When the Revolution started the British occupied New York City which further isolated Southold. There was much poverty and property was not maintained. Many residents left Southold during the Revolution and returned after the war only having to spend more to bring their property back to livable. Many of Long Island trees were stripped by the British to support life in New York City during the revolution.

So, who were our first ancestors to arrive in America? Where are they buried?

The buried part is easy. The Old Burying Ground cemetery of First Presbyterian church in Southold contains most of our original settlers. This includes William Purrier, Alice Purrier, Thomas Reeves, Peter Hallock, Thomas & Sarah Mapes, Henry

Tuthill II, and Bridget Tuthill. The problem is there are no headstones for any of these because of age and vandalism. Long Island was isolated from the rest of New England, so a head stone would have to be shipped in from Connecticut. William Wells, the lawyer, is the oldest head stone of our ancestors and is still standing in the Old Burying Ground. William died in 1671. The earliest death was Bridgett Tuthill or William King, both died in 1650 with no headstone. There is only one other headstone from the original founders related to us. That would be Barnabus Horton who die in 1680. He is said to have brought his gravestone with him to the New World: a 3' x 5' slab pre-engraved in England with all but his date of death. His grave site slab headstone has been elevated and very visible. Barnabus's grave is said to be the most visited grave in the Old Burying Ground.

Whom, among our relatives, was the first to arrive in America. Those who settled on Long Island did not come directly from England. They would have arrived two to five years before the 1640 settlement. Barnabas Horton and William Purrier arrive in America in 1635. Our earlies arrival to America never lived on Long Island. It was one generation earlier, my 9th Great Grandfather, Leonard Mapes esq. father of Thomas Mapes the surveyor. Leonard born in England in 1590. Leonard arrived in 1620, he was one of the 900 administrators for Virginia named by Captain John Smith and his occupation was that of land surveyor. He returned to England before 1625 and settled at Rowlesby County Norfolk where he was the high sheriff. There he died in 1638.

Chapter 31

Southold Exodus
(Escaping the British)

Picture the first thirteen families who bravely established settlements on Long Island. These were the pioneers, the ones who carved a life out of the wilderness. And among them, seven of those pioneering families are woven directly into our own family history, flowing through the bloodline of James M. Clark. James was the maternal grandfather of George and Robert Harris.

Although the women of the town did the spinning and much of the weaving, and all of the barnyard chores, their influence in the town was completely minus. Southold, and for that matter every other town in the new world, was a man's paradise. So great was the prestige of the male that when a town wished to punish a man for beating his wife, they did not bring a direct complaint but trumped up a charge of Sabbath breaking. Thirty-one men were licensed to sell rum to 3100 people. If there is any merit in the Kittredge theory of taverns as news depots, surely Southold of 1776 could not have been either thirsty or ignorant. It was to such a town that the news of an impending invasion came. The Presbyterian Church closed for six years during the Revolution.

With so much mention of war and its rumors, we may stop and consider the military aspects of the town. From the beginning there had been a military force called the Train Band, modeled after a similar force in England. Membership was obligatory, and the ages were from 16 to 60. Nothing but absolute decrepitude could excuse a settler from this duty. They met at eight o'clock every Monday morning and drilled for two hours, with time out for visits to the tavern and then back for another hour of drilling. The church was the armory, and as late as 1803 provisions were made in the new church for storing the arms of the militia, which had succeeded to the duties of the early Train Band. I have mentioned the weekly training because this was not the common custom in the other towns making up the County. The first Monday in the month was the accepted day for training, but the early Southolder's were so enamored of arms that they gave four days a month to this while their neighbors were only giving one. The ease with which Captain Thomas Terry raised a company of seventy-five men to serve in the Mohawk Valley campaign of 1760 plainly tells of the attitude of the town toward war.

A MUSTER ROLL OF CAPT PAUL REEVE CO

Draughted out of Coll Thomas Terry' Regiment Southold, August 5th, Southold, August 5th, 1776.

NAME	AGE	NAME	AGE
Paul Reeve, Capt.	42	Joshua Wells, Jr	16
John Corwin, Lt	41	Peter Downs	47
Joshua Benjamin, Lt	28	Jeremiah Corwin	41
Wheelock Booth, Serjt	34	Isaac Wells	30
Nathl _Conklin g, Serjt	36	Joshua Aldridge	25
Richard Steers Hubbard, Serjt	23	Peter Hallock	22
Jonathan Solloman (Salmon) Corp	33	Nathen Corwin	27
Constant Haven, Corp	45	Nathen Youngs	22
Joshua Wells, Corp	34	Nathen Corwin, Jr	16
James Pershall, Drum	22	Samuel Hudson	37
John Fradrik Hudson, Fif	20	Richard Benjamin	18
Nathl Overton	24	John Hallock	23
John Goldsmith	29	Jonathan Reeve	32
Joil Overton	21	Ruben Brown	39
Gilbert King	18	John Terry	22
John Goldsmith, Jr	21	Nathen Benjamin	17
Richard Drake	19	Ebenezer Hudson	17
Stephen Halsey	19	John Tuthill	46
Joseph Cleavland	17	Richard Wood	36
Ishmel Reeve	23	Richard Hallock	17
Ichabod Case	24	Amaziah Benjamin	35
Elijah Terry	19	Richard Brown	23
Calvin Horton	20	David Brown	29
David Benjamin	17	William Reeve	21
Luther Reeve	17+	Nathl Fanning	21
John Calven Wells	16	Amasa Pike	17
George Taylor	48	Daniel Terry	19
James Reeve (Ens)	24	John Parshall	19
Joshua Corwin	42	James Petty, Jr	24
John Griffin	38	Thomas Corwin	22

To the approaching invader, nothing was left- empty houses, closely mown fields, cropless acres, but nothing that could be of use. From 1776 until 1780, there was a steady stream of exiles, though no correct estimate has ever been made of their number. The Committee of Southold had anticipated the result of the Battle of Long Island by sending their cannon and ammunition to Saybrook. Following this, permission had been given to leave for the "main." 237 people were evacuated to the "main" (Connecticut) in September and October of 1776, others followed. That list included these names from our ancestors: (Capt.) Joseph Hallock 9, Joshua Horton 4, Richard Terey 11, Jonathan Wells 3, Joshua Reeves 3, Capt. (Barnabas) Horton 6, Barnabas Horton (Jr.) 4, Jonathan Horton 3. Other names in our ancestry line but not exiting Long Island at this time include Youngs, Tuthill, Benjamin, and Corwin.

With the departure of the first consignment of Refugees, the town began to know the hardships of war. Raiding parties of British soldiers began to appear and seize grain and cattle of those who had stayed behind. Those who had signed the Association on behalf of the Continental Congress found themselves in a bad way. Their crops and cattle were subject to seizure for their evident disloyalty.

While the loyal citizens of Southold were bearing up under their great load of troubles, military occupation, loss of crops, abuse both physical and verbal, in constant danger of hunger and disease, subject to raids from both friend and foe (numberless men of unquestioned devotion to the patriot cause had occasion to complain to Governor Trumbull that they had been plundered by their fellow patriots), and being constantly threatened with the fate that befell the Acadians, we may leave them and consider the fate of those who fled to the Connecticut side. Then hardships were the rule of the day. The inflexibility of the rules laid down to govern the Refugees made for hardships. In their haste, many had had little time to arrange their affairs on a satisfactory basis. Some in their haste had left crops unharvested; some had hidden stores of grain; some had come away without the needed utensils; some had buried money; some had debts falling due; and some had come away without money and had none in either place.

The enormous family holdings of the Corwin's, the Conklin's, the Wells, the Hortons, the Hallock's and so on through the list of those who had first come to the town were beginning to be broken up. Many had departed for Vermont, Orange County, the district about Utica, and some of the more hardy had even ventured to go among the hated Quakers of Pennsylvania. From out of Vermont, Orange County, Westchester and Dutchess came the grandsons of Southold in answer to their new country's call. The number of Conklin's would indicate that eventually they will dispute with the Tuthill's for the earth. They are our most prolific families. There are other good Southold names, notably: Horton, Dickinson, Wells, Griffing and Reeve that recur in the lists of other countries.

Why Orange County from Southold? Some Southold residents have left over the years prior to the Revolution. The Clarks appear to have migrated to Bedford NY then to Orange County. With the Revolution the British occupied New York City, exit from Long Island would be by sea through Connecticut. The British controlled the land east of the Hudson River and the Hudson River itself. Bedford was on the east side of the Hudson River. Newburgh, NY., was on the Hudson River west side and was the entry point to Orange County. There was no town or village or church that was to become Middletown and it was 25 miles west of the Newburgh and the Hudson River. Safer from the British but not so safe from Tories and Indians.

The First Congregational Church of Middletown, NY, established in 1785, has the highest spire downtown. Construction of its first building was a sign of Middletown becoming established as a village. 1785, was two years after the Revolution ended, before George Washington was President, the First Congregational Church was the first and only church in this vicinity for 40 years. Through 230 years we remain a Bible-centered evangelical church, affiliated with the Conservative Congregational Christian Conference. Middletown, NY was not incorporated into a city until 1888, a hundred years after the church. Middletown became a village in 1848.

"**Manual of the First Congregational Church of Middletown, NY**", states:

Says the Journal, " in 1640, we found Barnabas Horton, with his two children in New Haven, Connecticut, in company with Rev. John Youngs, William Wells, Esq. Peter Hallock, John Tuthill, Richard Terry, Thomas Mapes, Matthias Corwin, Robert Ackerly, Jacob Corey, John Conkling, Isaac Arnold, John Swazy, and John Budd; and on the 1ˢᵗ of October, 1640, assisted by the venerable John Davenport and Governor Eaton, they organized themselves into a Congregational Church and sailed to the East end of Long Island, now Southold. They had all been members of Puritan churches in England, and all had families with them, except Peter Hallock. On coming ashore, they all knelt down and engaged in prayer, Peter Hallock leading, as had been determined by lot."

Those participating in the Organization of the Middletown congregation were David Corwin and Mary Wells Corwin. David's mother Deborah Wells Corwin. Eli Corwin & Dorotha Horton Corwin, James Corwin and Mehitable Horton Corwin, James Reeve and Mary Corwin Reeve, were original members probably by letter from Long Island. The most prominent names evidently connect the Church with the Congregational Church at Southold, L.I. All the names shown in the organization of the Middletown church are in our ancestral lineage.

Basically, the people from Southold, Long Island who left their homes on Long Island in 1776, for the duration of the Revolutionary War established the Church in Orange County in what would become Middletown some 100 years later.

Chapter 32

Southold Long Island Families

Half of the founding families in the town of Southold, Long Island, are directly related to us. In addition, other families settled in and around Southold shortly after the 1640 landing. The founding families came to America at least two years prior to the settlement. Some of the other families (we are also related to came after the 1640 settlement but were actually in America before some of these founders. I will first cover our founding family connections then, those who came shortly after 1640.

Southold was the first town settled on Long Island. Long Island is larger than the state of Rhode Island and is 120 miles long east to west and over 25 miles north to south. Southold is on the East end. As more settlers arrived towns would develop westward toward NYC. Southampton, also in Suffolk County, was also founded in 1640. On the east end of Long Island, the land splits into a north fork and a south fork. Southampton is in the south fork. Small towns developing shortly after Southold are Cutchogue, Mattituck, Jamesport, Brookhaven, and Sweezyland.

The following are stories told about our ancestors who settled and lived on Long Island.

Rev John Youngs (8 GGF) b. 1598 d. 1672 wife Mary.
> For Rev. John Youngs there seems to be very little doubt that religious freedom was the reason he left his home in Southwold, England, to set out for Salem, MA which had been settled after the break-out of the Cape Anne trading post. From 1624-1628, settlers from Dorset, Somerset and Devon arrived in "Naumkeag" (Salem). On his arrival, Rev Youngs discovered others fleeing England like himself, had created an abundance of ministers and teachers in Salem. Finally, Youngs moved his band of eleven followers and their families to what would become Southold, Long Island. Landing on Oct 21, 1640, after two years of preparation in New Haven, CT.

Peter Hallock (9 GGF) b. 1595 England, d. 1689 wife?
> Peter was the only person of those who first settled in Southold to not bring his family. It is said that he was the first to set foot at the landing point. He purchased land from the Shinnecock Indians, in 1626 the tract of land, once called Oyster Ponds, and now called Orient. He returned to England to bring his wife to the new world and on coming back found that the Indians had

resold the land he had purchased. He then bought land extending from Long Island Sound on the North, to Peconic Bay on the south. He settled in Aquebogue, about two miles west of Mattituck village 6 miles west of Southold.

His first wife probably died in England and may have been ELIZABETH (MARGARET) YOUNGS, sister of Rev. John Youngs, but I have found no proof of this. They had one son, William Hallock, who was born in England. His second wife was the widow of a Mr. Howell. There was no issue born to this union.

(William, William, Zebulon, Zebulon, Zebulon, Mary, Chauncey Clark, James)

William Wells (8 GGF) b.1604 Norfolk, England, d.1671 Wife Mary Youngs 1619-1709.

Most accounts of the landing and settlement of Southold indicate he was a Lawyer and one of the more prominent. Those accounts also state that Peter Hallock was the only one traveling alone. This means that Mary was actually his second wife. William married Mary in 1654 in Southold and they had two boys William and Joshua, both were minors when he died. He was without any question endowed with rare gifts and accomplishments, competent, shrewd and equal to any emergency. Upon him the Colony of Southold relied chiefly on to make purchases of lands from the Indians. He was supposed to have been a professional Attorney. He never, himself, however appended the title to his name. He kept their records and drew up rules and regulations for their government, town meetings and Church Ordinances. His accumulation of lands was very large. Occabauk and Corchaug, large sections and many farms in the town of Riverhead. The Peninsula of Little Hog Neck, lying in Peconic Bay. His public service was extensive. He served as Deputy to the General Court at New Haven and as both Constable of Southold and as Southold Town Clerk. In 1665, after representing Southold in a Convention of Deputies assembled by the Governor, he was appointed High Sheriff of New Yorkshire on Long Island. Williams Headstone is the oldest grave marker on Long Island. (Jushua, Deborah, David Corwin, Eli, William, Mary, James Clark)

Barnabas Horton (9th GGF) b. 1600 Mowsley, England. 1680

Barnabas was a baker by trade. Box Tomb, Row 6, Stone 15. This box tomb marks the most-visited grave in The Old Burying Ground. Barnabus was a large, wise man. He did whatever needed to be done. Prominent in both Church and Town affairs, he became the settlement's go-to person.

Prospering here, he and his sons became richer than any other family in the settlement. He married three times. (Caleb, Hannah, Daniel Booth, Daniel, Bethiah, Mary Hallock, Chauncy Clark, James)

Henry Tuthill (9th GGF) b. 1612 England w. Bridget Elizabeth
John Tuthill, listed as one of the first 13 arrivals to Southold, was born in 1635 in Hingham, Massachusetts. Therefore, Henry Tuthill is more likely the first to settle in Southold. Henry's wife survived him and later became the wife of William Wells. (John, Hannah, Deborah Wells, David Corwin, Eli, William, Mary Clark wife of Chauncy Clark, James).

Richard Terry (8th GGF) b. 1618 London, England d. 1676 Southold, NY
Richard Terry sailed from England with his elder brothers, Thomas and Robert in 1635. Both Thomas and Robert subsequently ended up in Southold. In 1640 Richard was negotiating for land on Long Island. Richard Married Abigail Lines in 1650 in New Haven, CT. (Elizabeth, Nathan Benjamin, Nathan, Berthia, Matilda Sweezy, Mary Corwin, Chauncy Clark, James).

Thomas Mapes (8th GGF) b. 1626 Norfolk, England d. 1687 Southold, NY
Thomas Mapes was their surveyor. [1] The Town of Southold has this information on their website. Thomas Mapes was 18 years old in 1640. Thomas married Sarah Purrier in 1653 in Southold. (Naomi, Naomi Dickerson, Ruth Terry, Bethiah Booth, Mary Hallock, Chauncy Clark, James).

Mathias Corwin (9th GGF) b. 1596 Northampton, England d. 1658 Southold, NY
A grant for two acres of land in Ipswich, MA in 1634. He is considered the first Corwin to come to America. Settled Southold Long Island with Rev. Youngs in 1640. In 1665 he held 20 pieces of land in and around Southold.

Peter Hallock (9th GGF) b. 1585 England d. 1689 Mattituck, NY
William Hallock (8th GGF) b. 1610 Norfolk, England married Margret Howell about the time they arrived in Southold. William Hallock left a large personal estate in 1684. His will was dated Feb. 10, 1682, and proved October 21, 1684 leaving property to his wife, four sons & five daughters. To son William he left land near Southold. (Peter, William, William, Zebulon[1] , Zebulon[2], Zebulon[3], Mary, Chauncy Clark).
Zebulon[1] Did not evacuate Long Island at the start of the Revolutionary war. Three years later his son Zebulon[2], was granted permission by Connecticut to return to Long Island to care for his ailing Father. After the war ended

1783 many of the Hallock family moved to the area of Greenville, Orange County, NY. Zebulon[2], and Zebulon[3], followed after 1790 when the properties could be sold. Hard times in Greenville, NY. Zebulon[3], daughter Mary, married Hulet Clark and they had 7 children. When Mary was 32, she lost six of her youngest children within a 2-week period. Mary died two days later. They are in the Manning Cemetery in Greenville. Two weeks later Zebulon[3], and Zebulon[4], Mary's father and brother both died. They are buried 2 miles north as the first two bodies in the Hollock Blizzard Cemetery. One account says they were buried in the same grave. Within the next month five more Hallock children who lived in the same area were buried in the new Hallock cemetery. They were cousins once removed.

William King (9 GGF) Came to Massachusetts Bay in 1635 on the ship, "Marygould". He settled in Salem, with his wife Dorothy and several children. Deliverance (8th GGM) was born in Salem, MA in 1641. William died in Salem, but his wife Dorothy and daughter Deliverance live and died in Southold. Deliverance married John Tuthill (8th GGF). John Tuthill, Hannah, Deborah Wells, David Corwin, Eli, William, Mary, James Clark)

Charles Glover (9 GGF) The "Lion "arrived in Boston harbor on September 16, 1632 with passenger Charles Glover, a shipwright. Mary (8th GGM), daughter of Charles, was born in 1642 in Boston. She gets the award for the most children at 18. She married John Corwin Sr.

Sarah Foy (7 GGM) was born about 1665 in Southold, parents unknown. She married John Corwin II.

Thomas Reeve (8 GGF) b. 1611 Northamptonshire, England, d. 1665 Southold, NY Thomas arrived in America in 1635. Thomas married Mary Purrier daughter of William Purrier in Southold in 1845. There are 21 references to Thomas Reeve in the existing Town land records.

William Purrier (9 GGF) b. 1599 England d, 1676 Southold, NY.
Alice Knight (9 GGF) b. 1598 England d, 1671 Southold, NY (wife of William) William and Alice were from Olney, Buckinghamshire, the parish made famous by John Newton, slave trader and writer of the hymn "Amazing Grace". He sailed with his wife and three children from England on April first, 1635, on the ship "Hopewell". Their daughter Sarah married Thomas

Mapes in Southold. Their daughter Mary married Thomas Reeves. William came to Southold with his family between 1640 and 1650.

John Booth (8 GGF) b. 1629 England, 1689 Southold, NY
"Ensign" John Booth owned part of Shelter Island adjacent to Southold Long Island. John Booth first appears in a deed dated around 1652. (John, Daniel, Daniel, Bethiah Booth, Mary Hallock, Chauncy Clark, James).

Philemon Dickerson (8th GGF) 1593 – 1672 m. Mary Paine.
Philemon Dickerson sailed from Great Yarmouth, England May 10, 1637 on the ship "Mary Anne" to Salem, MA. Named as a servant of Benj. Cooper of Suffolk England. 1639 at Salem, a tanner; 1641, freeman of Salem; 1646-50 settled in Southold, L.I. in 1665, June 20, his will, probated, 28 Oct 1672. He married 1640-45 in Salem. (Peter, Naomi, Ruth Terry, Bethiah Booth, Mary Hallock, Chauncy Clark, James).

Edward Howell (9 GGF) 1584-1665
Edward had 7 children by Frances who died in England. He arrived in Boston in 1639 and had 3 more children by his second wife, Frances Paxton (9th GGM), who he married in 1640 in Southampton, Long Island. Shortly after arriving in Mecox, Howell announced he would build a mill for the grinding of grain, rye and wheat into flour. Until that date, all mills in what is now the State of New York, were wind-powered mills, due to the scarcity of lively streams. Wisely, Howell had chosen his Long Island land carefully to include a flowing stream and thus, in 1644, built what is now recognized as the first water-powered mill in the State of New York. It continued to supply flour for a wide area of communities for many generations after Howell's death. In fact, Edward built the mill so well it still stands today, 367 years later, in Water Mill, New York, near Mecox. The town of Water Mill chose its name to honor Edward Howell's mill. To further honor Howell for his many contributions to the State of New York, the Howell Family Arms (Gules, Three Towers) is engraved on the Great Western Staircase of the State of New York Capitol building in Albany, New York.

John Howell son of Edward (8 GGF) b. 1624 England, d. 1696, Southampton.
Major John Howell in his will directed that his remains be buried "by his father's sepulcher," and his tombstone bearing the ancestral arms still remain at the ancient burying ground in Southampton. Mathew Howell (Colonel), son of John, is buried with his father and grandfather in the Old

Southampton cemetery. His headstone is still standing. (Israel, Abigail, Mary Wickham, Eli Corwin, William, Mary, James Clark)

Joseph Wickham (6 GGF) 1662-1732.

Joseph arrived on Long Island at Sag Harbor perhaps 30 years after the settlement of Southold. The Wickham family history can be traced to the southern coast of England. By the middle of the 1600s the family had fled their homeland for religious reasons and sailed to New England. One of its members, Joseph Wickham, settled on Long Island and operated a tannery in Bridgehampton. In 1698, he moved to Cutchogue and bought the old English house and 160 acres of fertile farmland which ran from the main road south to Peconic Bay. Joseph Wickham farmed the land until his death in 1732, at which time the land was willed to his eldest son, Joseph Jr. That "Old House" has been restored and is now a landmark for visitors to Cutchogue. (Thomas b 1624 England, Joseph 1662 L.I. (6 GGF), Samuel, Mary, Eli Corwin, William, Mary, Chauncy Clark, James)

"Old House" was built in 1649 by John Budd in nearby Southold, then moved to Cutchogue in 1661. Purchased by Joseph Wickham in 1699. Past to his grandson Parker Wickham (February 28, 1727–May 22, 1785), famous for being a Loyalist politician during the American Revolution and who was banished from the State of

New York under dubious circumstances, owned and lived in the house. It was sold at auction. The house has been restored by the Historical society in Cutchogue.

John Swazey (7 GGF) b 1618, d. 1718 Aquebogue w. Katherine King 1625 - 1692

> The Quaker John Swazey came to this country from England and lived to the extreme age of 101 years. It may be said of him; he waged a double warfare. For he was assailed for his religious belief, and with his son John (6th GGF), driven out of Salem Mass. To seek refuge in a sparingly settled area on Long Island. Here he was allowed to remain, but not until he had submitted to the subscribed form of oath of Allegiance contrary to his religious convictions in about 1650. In his family at Southold the tenets of the Quaker or Friends faith continued down many generations. In the third generation Abigail Swazey married a John Hallock, both from Southold. His father William Hallock (8 GGF) disinherited him because he married into a family of "Friends or Quakers".

Chapter 33

When They Came to America

The following is a list that shows the first ancestor of our family line that came to America and the approximate date they arrived.

Name	Relationship	Arrival Place	from
John Swainston	grandfather	1910 NYC	South Shield, Eng.
Laura Annie Bell	grandmother	1914 NYC	South Shield, Eng.
Joseph Harris	1st GGF	1854 Tremont, PA	Wales
Lenah Williams	1st GGM	1854 Tremont. PA	Wales
Reese Williams	2nd GGF	1863 *Tremont, PA	Wales
Isaac Harris	2nd GGF	1863 *Illinois	Wales
Ann (unknown)	2nd GGF	1863 *Illinois	Wales
William Snyder	3rd GGF	abt. 1790 NY?	+
Phoebe Owen	3rd GGM	abt. 1790 ?	+
Peter Brown	7th GGF	>1650 Stamford	Hastings, Sussex, Eng
Elizabeth wife of Peter	7th GGM	>1650 Stamford, CT	England
Francis Purdy	7th GGF	>1650 Rye, NY	Norfolk, Eng.
Mary Brundage	7th GGM	>1650 Rye, NY	Ipswich,Suffolk,Eng
John Rundle	7th GGF	abt. 1650 Greenwich	Tonbridge, Kent, Eng
William Tyler	7th GGF	abt. 1650 Greenwich CT	+
Abigail Terrell	7th GGM	abt. 1650 Greenwich CT	+
Roger Park	6th GGF	>1680 Greenwich CT	+
Sophia Claes Jans	6th GGM	>1680 Greenwich CT	+
Daniel Strang	6th GGF	1680-1690	Orleans, France
Charlotte Marie Le Maistree	6th GGM	1680-1690	Orleans, France
Samuel Clark	8th GGF	1636 Wethersfield, CT	Devonshire, Eng
Hannah Fordham	8th GGF	1636 Wethersfield, CT	Devonshire, Eng
Susanna Treat	7th GGM	> 1650 Wethersfield, CT	+
Hannah Ayres	6th GGM	>1670 Stamford, CT	+
Sarah Dann	5th GGM	>1725 Bedford, NY	+
George Kniffen Jr.	8th GGF	abt. 1650 Rye, NY	Kniveton, Derbyshire,
Henry Whelpley	9th GGM	> 1644 Stratford, Ct	Norfolk, Eng
Rebecca Bulkeley	9th GGM	> 1644 Stratford, Ct	Staffordshire, Eng
Thomas Henry Merritt	9th GGF	>1634 Cambridge, MA	Ipswich, Eng.
Susanna Wolfenden	9th GGM	>1634 Cambridge, MA	England

Jane Sherwood	8th GGM	abt 1650 b. Fairfield CT	+
Johanna Sniffen	5th GGM	>1760 b. Bedford, NY	+
Peter Hallock	9th GGF	>1640 Southold, LI Southold, Eng.	
Margaret Howell	8th GGM	>1640 Southold, LI Southold, Eng.	
Thomas Reeve	8th GGF	>1645 Southold, LI , England	
Mary Purrier	8th GGM	>1645 Southold, LI England	
Martha wife of John Reeve	7th GGM	>1675 Southold, LI unknown	
John Booth	8th GGF	>1656 Southold, LI England	
Barnabas Horton	9th GGF	>1640 Southold, LI Mowsley,Leice, Eng.	
Mary Langton	9th GGM	>1640 Southold, LI England	
Father of Rose Holloway	7th GGF	>1670 b. Boston, MA +	
Joseph Emerson	8th GGF	>1656 b. MA +	
Mary Moody	8th GGM	>1656 b. York Maine +	
Philemon Dickerson	8th GGF	1637 Salem, MA/Southold, LI Eng.	
Thomas Paine	9th GGF	>1640 Salem MA Wrentham, Suffolk,	
Elizabeth Bloomfield	9th GGM	>1640 Salem MA Wrentham, Suffolk	
Thomas Mapes	8th GGF	>1640 Southold, LI Norfolk, England	
William Purrier	9th GGF	>1640 Southold, Olney, Bucking', Eng.	
Alice Knight	9th GGM	>1640 Southold,Olney, Buckinghamshir	
Thomas Terry	8th GGF	>1640 Southold, LI Barnet, Wiltshire,	
Mary Bigge	8th GGM	>1640 Southold,Biddenden,Kentshire.	
Sarah Moore	7th GGM	>1658 * Southold, LI	
Matthias Corwin	9th GGF	>1630Ipswich,MA Northampton, Eng.	
Margaret Shatswell	9th GGM	>1630Ipswich,MA/ Northampton, Eng.	
Charles Glover	9th GGF	1640/50 Southold, LI England	
Elizabeth Saunders	9th GGM	>1615? Salem, MA +	
Sarah Foy	7th GGM	>1665 Southold, LI +	
William Wells	8th GGF	1635 Southold LI Norwich,Norfolk, Eng	
Mary Marie Youngs	8th GGM	>1640 Southold, LI Norwich, Eng.	
Henry Tuthill II	9th GGF	>1635 Southold, LI Tharston, Norfolk,	
Bridget Elizabeth	9th GGM	>1635 Southold, LI Tharston, Norfolk,	
William King	9th GGF	>1641 Salem, MA England	
Dorothy Hayne	9th GGM	>1641 Salem, MA England	
Abigail Davis	5th GGM	>1760 Southold LI +	
Thomas Wickham	7th GGF	>1662 Wethersfield, CT +	
Sarah Goodrich	7th GGM	>1662 Wethersfield, CT Bassingbourn,	
John Howell I	8th GGF	>1647 Southampton, Westbury Manor	
Susan Mitchell	8th GGM	>1647 Southampton St. Jn's Parish, Halifax	

Thomas Halsey   8th GGF   >1650 Hayground, suffolk, NY

* Indicated person was not the first but the most distant ancestor arriving
+ indicates the line has not been established to an arrival in America.
Note: Martha Jones wife of Reese Williams may have died in Wales?
Note: Ancestors who settled in Southold, LI came to America earlier than the
1640 founding of Southold. Many that are shown as Southold came indirectly
through MA or CT.

Chapter 34

Cemeteries & Headstones - a Testimony

In our ancestors lives from 1640 until the late 1800s, a "Last will and Testament" was the common way to transfer assets to the next generation. Somehow today we have left out the testimony and merely give a last will. Those testimonies are interesting to read as the deceased expressed his faith in Christ and the hope that is set before him.

The next closest thing we find in the form of a testimony is a head stone. Today's headstones have also left out the testimony. Some old headstones have lost their effects as we seldom visit these burial sites, and some stones are no longer legible due to age and wear.

Where are our family headstones:

George & Elizabeth Harris		Memorial Park, Battle Creek, MI
Joseph & Ada Harris		Memorial Park, Battle Creek, MI
Cornelia (Snyder) Clark		Memorial Park, Battle Creek, MI
John & Laura Swainston		Memorial Park, Battle Creek, MI
James M. Clark		Rose Hill Mem. Park, Tulsa, OK
Joseph & Lenah Harris	*	Cottonwood Cemetery, Braceville, IL
Isaac & Ann Harris	*	Cottonwood Cemetery, Braceville, IL
Reese Williams		M.E. Church cem. Tremont, PA
Chauncey & Mary Clark		Hillside Cemetery, Middletown, NY
Hulet H. Clark		Union Cemetery, Orange Co, NY
Mary Clark (Wife of Hulet)		Manning Cemetery, Orange Co. NY
Zebulon Hallock III		Hallock / Blizzard Cem. Orange Co. NY
Caleb & Jennifer Clark		Manning Cemetery, Orange Co. NY
William & Matilda Clark		Hillside Cemetery, Middletown, NY
Eli & Mary Corwin		Hillside Cemetery, Middletown, NY
William D. & Eliza Snyder	*	Putnam Cemetery, Greenwich, CT
Nehemiah Brown Jr.		M.E. Church Cemetery, Round Hill
Nehemiah & Sophia Brown		Burying Hill Cemetery, Round Hill, CT
Barnabas Horton (9GGF) 1680		Church Cemetery, Southold, LI
Multiple ancestors from Long Island		Multiple Church Cemeteries, in LI

    *Indicated there is no headstone

About the Author

David Joseph Harris was born on July 20, 1946 in Marshall, Michigan – the third son of five born to George and Elizabeth Harris. He grew up on the farm where the five rowdy boys brought much life by shooting each other with BB guns, jumping out of the barn, wrestling, and playing with Grandpa Joe who lived with them. David became an Eagle scout.

Early on, David would walk to his one-room schoolhouse. Not particularly studious as a youth, he did eventually graduate with a Bachelor's degree later in life from Spring Arbor College.

His mother took him to Convis Union Methodist Church where as a shy young

Figure 10. David, Mary Ann, Mark, Amy in 1976

man he met and later married Mary Ann Keathley on September 23, 1967 in Battle Creek, Michigan where he lived most of his life. They had two children, Mark David Harris – born August 3, 1969 and Amy Marie Harris – born July 24, 1972.

Now retired, David worked at Eaton Corporation in Marshall, Michigan as a quality assurance engineer most of his life. For ten years following retirement, he and Mary Ann served in the SOWER organization, traveling the United States in their fifth-wheel helping various Christian organizations however they could – usually with construction projects. They now live in Anderson, Indiana near Amy's family and winter in Bradenton, Florida.

David took an interest in genealogy and dedicated decades to this work. Many of his family vacations were centered around particular cemeteries or libraries tracking down a new family line. He did the legwork of pouring through microfilm and microfiche. Today's internet makes this work much easier. He probably pursued genealogy because he realizes the deep value of family.

A man of faith, David and Mary Ann taught children in Sunday School for many years. He and Mary Ann deeply love and invest well in their children, grandchildren, and now great grandchildren. David will often be found helping with DIY projects

Figure 11. David and Mary Ann in 2023

around their homes, playing card games, playing pickleball, golfing, or even wrestling with his great-grandchildren. His grandchildren cannot believe that he reports he grew up as a shy young man because he is often now one of the bigger personalities in the room.

He often says he wants the following testimony written on his tombstone when he passes:

"The King of Kings calls me His own."

www.ingramcontent.com/pod-product-compliance
Lightning Source LLC
Chambersburg PA
CBHW041601260326
41914CB00011B/1344